CW00927232

The Pet Gundog

A common sense approach to dog training

2nd Edition

Lez Graham

Published by Trained for Life.
Copyright © Lez Graham.

First published by AuthorHouse 22/06/2010
2nd Edition published by Trained for Life December 2011
ISBN 978-0-9570051-1-2

Photographs by Nick Ridley
Printed and bound in Great Britain

A catalogue record for this book is available from the British Library.

All rights reserved.

No part of this book may be reproduced, stored in a retrieval system, or transmitted by any means without the written permission of the author.

The information and recommendations in this book are given without any guarantees on behalf of the author who disclaims any liability with the use of this material

Contents

This book is dedicated to all of those who, like me,
share their home with a glorious gundog

Foreword

This is a book which has been needed for a long time; it does exactly what it says in the title.

'The Pet Gundog' is intended for people that own a dog from the working Gundog Breeds. And in fact the majority of Gundogs are kept first and foremost as pets and secondly for their abilities as working dogs.

Lez Graham is very much a modern and progressive dog trainer; she has blended traditional training methods with the latest views and methods of a behaviourist encouraging the reader to understand how your dog thinks, behaves and reacts in all sorts of situations both inside the home and once you take him out for a walk.

This knowledge is essential if you are to be successful when taking on a dog from the modern Gundog Breeds. These dogs are highly specialised which means that they are exceptionally good at doing what they are bred to do, hunt and retrieve.

Reading this fascinating book will give The Pet Gundog trainer a much deeper understanding of day to day management of this breed type.

Throughout the book Lez explains the need to ensure that the dog, young or old, is given clear boundaries. The chapters on practical training explain how the dog sees the world and its surroundings and details how to train and teach him to co-exist amongst his human pack, in doing this you also lay the foundations for future Gundog work.

Lez Graham is a highly experienced trainer of dogs, I know as I have been privileged to observe and assess her dog training classes, her skill and depth of knowledge in the subject is shared with us throughout this book and I believe that any student of Dog Training will thoroughly enjoy and benefit from its contents.

Howard Kirby
Lains Shooting School and Mullenscote Gundogs

Acknowledgements

I strongly believe that people come into your life for a reason, either for you to learn something from them or for them to learn something from you. Sometimes it's a fleeting meeting and other times they remain in your life enriching the fabric of what makes you, you.

I have many, many people to thank for helping me along the way, not just as a dog trainer and behaviourist but in the role that led to this one, as a kinesiologist and Touch for Health Instructor, working with people, dogs and horses. It was my former occupation that gave me the depth of knowledge on the mechanics of movement and the psychology of people, predators and prey animals, as well as an appreciation of energy and how it affects us and our dogs.

My gratitude is expressed in the order of people arriving in my life. To my husband I owe the greatest debt. He has had to listen to me over the years going through various learning curves and probably knows as much, if not more, about dogs and the way they think, move and communicate, than a lot of trainers I've met over the years. He has enriched my life without compare.

Sandy Gannon and Jeff Abel, for always being there, even after I left the field of complementary health to specialise in dog behaviour; and for always showing an interest in my 'dog world'.

Jill Stagg for breeding my beautiful Labrador Bart and for being my mentor on all things to do with shooting and country life, from naming the various trees we'd stand under gossiping to explaining why the New Forest ponies tails are cut at different lengths.

For all the dog trainers who've helped me find my own way; Sandra & Wayne Williams, Noel Hutchinson, Dee Steadman and for my colleagues who've not only given moral support whilst writing this book but are also doing so much for dogs and dog owners; Howard Kirby, Colin Tennant, Ross McCarthy, Charlie Clarricoates... and of course all the other trainers and behaviourists that I work with.

To Carol, Charlotte, Nick and Sally for allowing me to include photos of their gorgeous gundogs; Jasper the large Munsterlander, Topo the Spanish water dog, Harry the Cocker spaniel and last but not least Beanie the Springer spaniel.

My appreciation goes to Nick Ridley, not only for the superb photos but for his help and guidance also; to Sue Jackson at Quest Gundog Training Equipment for supplying me with dummies and the like and to Robert Pownall of The Scurry Bandits.

And finally great thanks must be afforded to 'The Gundoggers' who train with me week in week out, in rain, wind, sun, snow and rain. It rains a lot on gundog days which is why I mentioned it twice. Without my gundoggers and their dogs I wouldn't have learned anywhere near as much as I have and I certainly wouldn't have had as much fun doing it.

Introduction

This book is for anyone who has a gundog breed living at home with them as a pet; you may, or may not, be interested in taking him out on a shoot but want to know more about what makes your gundog tick and how to get the best out of him.

The idea for this book came from my gundog training classes for pet owners, which in turn came from the amount of gundogs that I saw as a dog behaviourist that were living in the home environment, bored and destroying the home or hyperactive and out of control.

Before we go any further however, I'd like to apologise to all the owners of gundog 'girls', having two boys I tend to refer to dogs that I don't know as he. Referring to he/she, or even s/he, all the way through would be tiresome and no doubt irritating, and so I'm doing us all a favour and sticking with what I know best... dogs of the male persuasion. Likewise using the word 'dog' in place of your dog's name. I use the generic term 'dog' as it saves me writing "your dog's name followed by the command..." which I'm sure would become very tedious in a very short space of time. Anyway, onwards and upwards as they say!

A gundog is quite simply a dog that was originally used, to either find live game, to retrieve game that was shot, or both. For this reason the gundog group is generally split into Retrievers, Spaniels (Hunting Retrievers), Pointers and Setters and Hunt Point Retrievers (HPRs).

The Retrievers include breeds like the Labrador retrievers, Golden retrievers, Chesapeake Bay retrievers, Flatcoated retrievers, Nova Scotia Duck Tolling Retrievers... you get the idea. These are, as the name implies, the dogs that bring back the spoils, although they can be used to flush, retrieving is what's 'in their blood'.

Spaniels or Hunting Retrievers as they're referred to, include for example Springer spaniels, Cocker spaniels, Field spaniels, Clumber spaniels etc, hunt to find live game to flush, put it up to be shot and then bring it back for the table. Although the Hunting Retriever can be used to pick up, they're more often than not thought of as beaters dogs as they can get into the smaller places to put up game (and retrieve it from); natural at quartering you'll see them running back and forwards ahead of you on walks totally 'in their noses' doing what comes naturally.

The Pointers and Setters group would include the English Pointer, Irish setters, Gordon setters and so on. The Pointers and Setters have their origins very much in England, Scotland and Ireland. Their job is to find game, freeze or point at it until instructed to either flush or allow their handler to deal with it.

Hunt Point Retrievers (HPRs) are generally European dogs that became more popular after the second world war and include German Short-haired Pointers, Italian Spinones, Large Munsterlanders, Vizlas, Weimaraners and so on.

The Pointers and Setters and the HPR group, although having different origins have similar roles on the shooting field, and with the advent of the Gundog Club, the groups have been merged under the HPR banner, probably for that reason. The Kennel Club however keeps, and refers to, the groups in their truest form.

For me it's the HPRs that are different to the other gundog groups as you can't train 'the point'; they either have it or they don't. The HPRs will find the game and 'point' at it, on command put it up to be shot and then bring it back.

So that's the types of gundogs, but I would be surprised if as many as half were trained as such. Why? Well because they make such great family pets and families these days tend not to go out and shoot their lunch, preferring to go to Waitrose or Sainsbury's instead.

The Gundog is a superb companion (I have two, a black lab and a golden retriever); easy going, reasonably easy to train, fun, powerful, outgoing and biddable.... that's when their energy is channelled. Leave them to their own devices and you'll get a large'ish dog that creates his own fun, for example being chased around the garden with your sexy undies in his mouth when mother-in-law comes to visit; outgoing as in he runs up to everyone and covers them in slobber and muddy paw-prints; powerful, yes, they can drag a fully grown man down the street and not break into a sweat; is biddable with everyone except you... sound familiar?

Welcome to the world of the pet gundog...

Gundogs are us... OK !

So you've got a pet gundog?

Congratulations, you are the proud owner of a highly intelligent, high energy working dog.

Some of the many things that inspired me to run gundog classes and also to write this book were the amount of gundogs that I was seeing as a Canine Behaviour Practitioner that were intelligent and eager to please and yet were totally dominating their owners and destroying the home – why?

Basically, because they were bored out of their minds.

Here were these wonderful creatures that had been bred, generation after generation, to work alongside man, doing his bidding and flushing, pointing at and retrieving his lunch. Instead of doing what they were bred for they were being forced into sedentary lives, being screamed at for picking up the remote control and banished to the garden to amuse themselves.

Don't kid yourself if you've got a 'show' type either. The first dog show in England wasn't until 1859 and then it was about function not form... The Kennel Club wasn't formed until 1873 with the first stud book published in 1874. Ever wondered why Crufts is held in March? To allow for the dogs out in the shooting field to recover from a winter of hard work and get scrubbed up.

The Gamekeepers, or Special Working Gundog, class is still very popular and is for, funnily enough, gundogs that work.

Dogs have worked alongside man since before records began. In the middle ages the dogs were armoured up and were used to defend caravans; Napoleon used dogs as sentries to warn his troops of potential attack; Attila the Hun used the precursors of the Mastiff and Talbot breeds; in 1904 ambulance dogs were trained by a British dog fancier in Imperial Russia; during the Gulf War almost 2,000 highly trained German Shepherds were used by the French forces to protect their supplies, aircraft and of course their troops.

There's just no getting away from it, dogs over the millennia have been bred to work; show type or not... that's a working dog you've got sharing your living room.

Indoors or out?

Most working gundogs live outdoors, that is gundogs that go out on shoots. Some pet gundogs spend their time in the kennel during the day and in the home at night but the majority of them are indoor dogs, living inside 24 hours a day.

Does it matter? No. Unless, of course, you want a field trial champion and then yes it does matter.

When I speak to fellow gundog trainers they all agree, training an indoor dog to be a working gundog is much, much tougher than training an outdoor dog. Why?

Well, when you have a kennelled dog you are their excitement for the day. Everything that is exciting in your dog's life revolves around you and your opening of the kennel door. Does that dog want to please you – you bet. The dog will be thrilled to be with you and will no doubt be jumping out of his skin "what we doing?" "where we going?" "how fast would you like to get there" "now" "what about now" and so on, with the dog's tail going twenty to the dozen.

Now, compare that to the indoor dog. Every day thousands of smells around the home compete for your attention. Combine that with the kids running around generating excitement, the TV going, the radio on, the doggie toybox in the corner, the owner who chats away endlessly "think I'll make a nice cup of tea now Gromit" and so on... the dog tunes out to the voice and makes his own amusement. In effect, the indoor dog doesn't need the owner to provide excitement, he has that already.

That doesn't mean to say you can't have an excellent working dog that lives indoors. Both my dogs live indoors and work over the winter and the lady who bred my Labrador has an excellent working bitch which lives indoors. It can be done – it just requires discipline, more on the part of the owner rather than the dog; discipline not to have a running commentary on every aspect of your day and discipline to enforce commands first time (more on that hot topic later).

4

At the end of the day your dog is a pet and must fit in with your lifestyle and the lifestyle of your family. If it suits you to have your dog indoors then do so... your dog, your choice.

What to look for in a gundog... trials v pet?

First and foremost, regardless of whether you want a pet, a trials champion or a good beaters dog or pickers up dog, the most important thing is health. Health is the be all and end all in any dog you'll ever get. Check the problems that your chosen breed is known for and make sure the line you go for is clean and that the parents have been tested.

The Labrador for example has joint problems. My breeder gets hips and elbows scored and won't breed from a bitch, or choose a sire, which has a poor score. Likewise with the eyes – the eyes must be checked for Progressive Retinal Atrophy (PRA). Research your chosen breed and ask the breeder if the line your dog is coming from has any problems, better yet ask a different breeder if the line you're interested in has an inherited problem; you may get a more comprehensive answer.

The next thing after health is temperament. You want a dog to have a good temperament. Any aggressive tendencies should be avoided like the plague – remember you're going to have to take things out of your dogs mouth at some point and I'm sure you'd like to keep all of your fingers. There are a number of reasons why I love my breeder, first of all she's a gentle but firm handler and secondly she won't breed from a bitch until she's proved she's capable on the field AND has shown to be sound mentally and emotionally with people and other dogs.

You now have to consider what, if anything, you want to do with your dog:

If you want to run tests or trials then go for a dog with a trials pedigree. If it's your first dog then going for a dog with Field Trial Champions (FTCh) all the way back to day one is probably a bad idea, it will run rings around you – these dogs generally need experienced handlers, with a no-nonsense approach to training and nerves of steel.

If you want a pet gundog to specifically take out on shoots, go talk to the local gamekeeper and ask if he can recommend any of the dog handlers that work for him that you can talk to about getting a working dog. Remember you don't always have to go for a puppy; sometimes it's easier to buy a trained dog or a dog that has been trained in obedience and basic gundog work (classed as a part trained dog) so that you don't have to learn everything in one hit.

If you want a pet gundog that at some point you may want to train to pick up/ flush, then look at how the parent works (if you can) or talk to the breeder about what previous litters have done, for example do they work? Are they pets? Do they do agility or flyball? Do they trial?

You're looking for a dog that has drive and a willingness to work for you but won't become obsessive or try to bully you.

What about the dog that shares your home? Well hopefully the above will have given you an insight into the type of breeding you have sitting at your feet and the rest of this book will help you get to grips with training him.

All gundogs, regardless of whether they're field trial champions or show dogs, have been bred to work... somewhere down their line they were working dogs. The trialling dogs come from generations of FTChs, the working dogs tend to come from working dogs and the pets tend to come from both as well as those bred for the show ring. The times are changing however and the Kennel Club are looking more to function and movement in their breed standards and so, I suspect, more 'working stock' will be bred into the show dogs blurring the differences even more.

Shoots, trials, tests and then some

There are loads of things you can do with your trained pet gundog. I can remember when I first got my Labrador feeling totally lost in a sea of jargon... when is a trial not a trial? What's the difference between a scurry and a test? Is there one? What's a rough shoot? The questions were endless... luckily I had a very good mentor and used to bend her ear under the trees waiting for the 'time to work' whistle to go.

As a gundog trainer I regularly get phone calls from people who have got gundogs of 'a certain age', (generally between 6 and 8 months old) saying they want to train their dog to do field trials. They've been to the local game fair and have seen gundogs working in the demonstration ring. "Fantastic" is normally my response, "do you know what a field trial is?"

As we talk it generally transpires that what they mean is they want to train their dogs to retrieve dummies, do scurries and generally have fun with their dog. The information that follows is a brief description of things that you can do with your pet gundog if you feel so inclined.

The Shoot

There are different kinds of shoots and every one of them is run in its own is way. I went on a shoot last season with a couple of the girls who've been training their dogs with me; we were standing out of the way in the picking up line listening to the beaters pushing the birds forward. All three of us had been on different shoots but this was the first time together. One of the girls, who'd only been on one other shoot asked "do the beaters always make that much noise?" "Yes" was one reply, "no" was the other.

I work my dogs at two shoots; one is a formal driven commercial shoot whilst the other is a local reasonably informal driven syndicated shoot (that is a group of people who combine resources to rent the shoot).

Walked up

Many driven shoots have elements of walking-up, especially towards the end of the season when the birds are scarce on the ground. In a walked-up shoot a line of Guns, generally around 100 yards or so apart, will walk along with their gundogs (generally spaniels) flushing birds as they find them. Once a bird is shot, the line is halted while the game is retrieved. At a signal from the gamekeeper the line will proceed and shooting will re-commence.

Sometimes a walked up shoot is also referred to as a rough shoot, however, on a rough shoot the amount of game available is less and sometimes no game is placed down in preparation for the shoot, rather you rely on natural habitat and weather to provide lunch, in whatever form it takes.

Driven

A Driven shoot is the traditional shoot that everyone pictures in their mind when they think of pheasant shooting in Britain, the one that is portrayed on countless paintings. The favourites on a driven shoot are pheasants and partridges, both birds providing their own challenges to the guns. The birds are driven by the beaters and their dogs towards the waiting guns, which are lined up at pegs. It may sound very simple making birds fly up but there is a definite knack to getting the birds in the air at the right time, in the right direction and at the right height for the waiting line of guns.

The shoot is made up of a number of drives, depending on the size of the shoot and can be anywhere between three and eight drives in day.

Beaters, Guns and Pickers-up

As you may have guessed from the above the Beaters are a group of people who flush the game forward for the waiting Guns. On a signal from the gamekeeper, the beaters move forwards with their dogs through woodland or cover flushing or 'putting up' birds in their path. The beaters dog is traditionally the spaniel.

The Gun is the person that shoots the gun rather than the gun itself… complicated but simple! At the beginning of each day, or sometimes each drive, the Guns draw a straw to see which peg, or position in the shooting line, they'll be using. Most Guns tend not to have dogs out with them, concentrating instead on shooting; when they do have a dog with them, the dog will be referred to as a 'peg dog' and is whichever breed the Gun prefers. The Guns do not start shooting until they hear the 'start shooting' marker which is either a whistle or a horn used by the gamekeeper.

The pickers-up and their dogs stand at a distance behind the Guns. When they hear the second whistle they know that the shooting has ended for that drive and they can release the dogs to do their job. The younger or less experienced dogs are generally kept on lead until the second whistle goes, whereas the more experienced and 'steady' dogs are sat off lead by the handler. These are the dogs that are sent for a pricked bird (injured but not killed) before the second 'end of shooting' whistle goes. An inexperienced dog is never sent for a pricked bird as it can frighten the dog and make it apprehensive on game.

The Gamekeeper

Last but definitely not least there is the gamekeeper, who not only organises the rearing of the young birds but deals with the administration involved in the shooting day, from taking the booking to organising beaters and pickers-up and keeping everything running smoothly on the day. It's one of the most stressful jobs I'm aware of as when it goes well no-one comments but when it goes wrong, for whatever reason, the gamekeeper is in the proverbial firing line.

I can remember my first shoot as if it was yesterday. I hadn't really planned on doing anything with my Labrador other than having a really well trained dog. When he was about 5 months old I went on a shoot with his breeder and watched his mum work; that was it I was totally hooked. To see the dogs working in the way that they've been bred to was just awesome. It doesn't matter what discipline I do with my dogs or how much they enjoy it, nothing lights up their eyes in quite the same way as picking up, be that on a shoot or just training with canvas dummies.

Field Trials

Fields trials are serious business and are based on either a walk-up shoot or a driven shoot. They are run by gundog clubs around Britain according to the Kennel Club Field Trial Regulations and are held during the shooting season. Your dog needs to be a pedigree and registered with the Kennel Club.

Nothing is staged and therefore your dog needs to be competent retrieving feather and fur, and, your dog needs to be incredibly steady. Steady enough to walk to heel off lead or sit by your side while guns are going off, dogs are flushing birds, hares are running past and other dogs are retrieving; all without a command being given. Oh, and your dog needs to be silent. Any whining, yipping, yapping or barking and you will be asked to close the gate on your way out.

Field trials can be either one day stakes which normally have between 10 and 16 dogs, or two day stakes which are generally 20 to 24 dog events. All field trials are seriously over-subscribed and so the entrants are decided by a draw.

Apart from the standard of training and dedication involved and the luck being picked in the draw, there's also the travelling around the country to get to the trials as well as the massive expense in doing so. To achieve the heady recognition of owning a Field Trial Champion (FTCh) you need to have won at least three days worth of Open stakes (2 two days stakes, 3 one day stakes or 1 two day stake and 2 one day stakes): no wonder the FTCh on a dogs pedigree is so highly sought after and held in such high regard around the world.

Working Tests

Working tests are fairly serious and are run by gundog clubs around Britain according to the Kennel Club Regulations for Gundog Working Tests (GWTs) and are held throughout the year, although primarily in the summer in preparation for the shooting season. Your dog needs to be a pedigree and registered with the Kennel Club.

Nothing is shot during a working test, although cold game may be used as well as canvas dummies. Mimicking a shoot as closely as possible your dog is expected to retrieve marked and hidden (blind) dummies at distance and over obstacles.

There are four categories of Working Gundog Tests:

Open, which is open to all dogs of a specified breed although preference may be given to dogs which have been placed at a certain level at a Field Trial.

Novice, which is restricted to dogs which haven't gained a place above a certain level in a Gundog Working Test.

Puppy, which is restricted to dogs of a specific breed and less than eighteen months of age.

Unclassified, which is open to all breeds but restrictions are determined by the group, club or society that is running the test.

There is a little bit of rivalry between working test handlers and scurry handlers; the working test handlers generally thinking that scurries are for amateurs or that they'll 'break' your dog for bigger and better things.

Scurries

A gundog scurry is a fun event which is open to the general public regardless of breed and ability and can be found at Country fairs up and down the country from local to national throughout the year.

Scurries are a test of speed combined with a retrieve and range from the novice scurry where your dog is timed on picking up two thrown dummies, to the skill stretching pot black where your dog has to retrieve dummies that are coloured like and retrieved in the order of a game of snooker and anything in between.

The most common scurries are:

The novice or Long retrieve, which is a dummy thrown in clear view approximately 50 yards away, retrieved against the clock.

Two dummy pickup, which is just two dummies thrown, one to the right and one to the left; both dummies to land prior to retrieving, against the clock.

Up & over, two dummies to be retrieved over obstacles, against the clock.

Partridge pen, two pens that your dog needs to jump into to collect a dummy for you – yup it's against the clock.

Dummy launcher, where your dog retrieves a dummy fired from a launcher, also against the clock.

Depending upon the amount of space available at the fair, you may also find the Clock scurry where twelve dummies are placed in the formation of the clock face and you have to retrieve at least four, sometimes you'll be told the order to send your dog sometimes you won't.

The top scurry for the serious competitor is the Dog and Gun scurry where you get to shoot six clays and your dog retrieves three to four dummies which are placed on the field whilst you are shooting.

Although there are generally prizes in the scurries, they really are all about having some fun with your dog. The only pressure when entering a scurry is the pressure you put on yourself.

As you can see, scurries are a lot less formal than the working tests mentioned above, but like most things with your pet gundog, it's your choice in what direction you want to take your dog and what you want to do with him.

It's a Dog's Life

Man has exploited dogs for years… now they're exploiting us.

Those big brown puppy dog eyes, the expressive forehead and the happy wagging tail; combine that with the media and we have the irresistible Andrex puppy and Lassie coming home; mix it with a large pinch of human nature and we think our dog understands every word we say, treat it like a best friend and confidante and then take it personally and act broken hearted, when, quite literally in some cases, it 'bites the hand that feeds it'.

Our attitude towards dogs has changed dramatically over the last couple of decades… something that I personally tie in with the advent of central heated houses and the price of household goods coming down. That may seem like quite a leap but in the old days (and now I sound like my Mam) it was a case of shutting doors to keep the heat in and the cold out; the dog had to ask to be allowed in or out. Sofas and settees cost six months worth of salary and no-one was going to have a smelly wet dog on them – they stayed on the floor. Also back then it was customary for the dogs to be out roaming most of the day so it was tired… and a tired dog is a happy dog or more importantly a dog that's not looking for mischief. Also people tended to get a dog when the wife gave up work to have children and so the dog was the bottom of the list after dealing with household chores, husband and children.

Nowadays, furniture is cheap (or at least a lot more affordable), houses are warm, people are putting off having families until much later and having dogs as surrogate children, oh and the laws have changed in relation to dogs roaming free on the streets. All these changes make for an under walked over privileged dog.

We need to get inside our dogs head to understand what it means to be a dog and start treating them like dogs again, only then will we truly fulfil their needs and have the relationship with them that we used to have and, if we were honest with ourselves, crave.

Take me to your Leader !

The concept of leadership is sadly mistaken by lots of people. Unfortunately it seems to be interpreted as to bully or boss around whomever or whatever you're trying to lead.

Dominance has also become a dirty word through misuse...

All dominance means is "the disposition of an individual to assert control in dealing with others", while leadership means "an act or instance of leading; guidance; direction" not an awful lot between them really. So how do we apply dominance and leadership with our dog ?

Well, we, the human, have control over all the things that the dog values in life... food, water, the den (home), toys, beds etc., This automatically makes us an important member of the group, the leader if you like. However, the human, being human and a sucker for anthropomorphising everything we come across from walls (they have ears don't you know!) to dogs, puts human emotions on the dog and not only treats the dog like a human in a fur coat but is inconsistent with it. The dog is allowed to sit on the sofa at the same level as the human, but maybe only when it's clean and dry. Treats are fed by the human as-and-when but for no apparent reason as far as the dog can make out (no doubt it gave the human "that look").

The dog, like most other animals on the planet has a "what's in it for me attitude" and begins to test its boundaries by taking a bit of control for itself. If the dog is not reprimanded (no doubt it has perfected "the look") it takes even more liberties and the human not only allows it, they actively encourage it by allowing the dog to pull on the lead, jump up at other humans and onto the furniture. The dog now realises that there are no boundaries and that it can do anything that it chooses while the owner unwittingly encourages it to do so.

The dog knows (being a dog after all and not a human in a fur coat) that there should be a strong leader in its pack and, with all these privileges being afforded to them by the human it must be them. Not many dogs will want this status for themselves, most are far happier if the human sorts out the day to day what to do when and for how long and with whom nonsense. All that the dog wants to know is where it stands within the pack. From a failure on the owner's part to be a responsible leader, the dog is forced into taking the role for himself, resulting in a seriously confused and probably stressed out dog with behavioural problems.

We need to stop putting our story on to everything and be the leader that our dog not only wants us to be but needs us to be. Dogs know how to be dogs and can play, 'smooch', get up close and personal and yet still know the order in life... it's us humans that put a spanner in the works by 'feeling' - "I can't tell pooch off, he won't love me anymore" or "if I don't let him on the settee he'll stop coming to say hello" or "I can't tell him not to do that because he looks so sad". A lot of it is fear of rejection by their dog if they reinforce boundaries, so many owners don't.

Now, a dog knows another dog will still 'love' them even as they are reprimanding them - all you have to do is watch a dog overstep the line in play; they might get a sharp growl or even a nip and they'll be straight back in there 2 seconds later but showing less exuberance and more restraint. They live in the moment and don't worry about what others think, they respond instinctively - a bit like grandma smacking the back of your hand when you reach for something you're not allowed... they're old enough and wise enough to know that a tingling hand won't stop you from loving them, just stop you from doing the action again (well in front of them anyway).

For me, with dogs, it's about self respect... I'm not going to allow my dogs to jump all over me and hurt me and nick my food and mess up my place. I expect them to be respectful of me and my personal space and if they're not I do something about it - doesn't mean I don't love them and they don't love me, it just means I have boundaries and they know it... when you have boundaries you don't need to tell your dog what it can and can't do all the time, you just need to remind them occasionally (like the dog overstepping the line in play).

Pack Mentality

Although we all know that the dog is a dog and not a wolf (or a person in a fur coat for that matter!), they do share, not only a dim and distant relative, but DNA to within 0.2% of the grey wolf, have brains that are physically identical in all but size and can mate with a wolf producing viable offspring. The name of the dog was actually changed in 1993 to Canis Lupis Familiaris (from Canis Familiaris) to reflect the fact that it is a sub-species of the wolf.

Over the years extensive breeding programmes by man have changed not only the look of the dog but also refined specific traits so that the modern dog, in certain breeds, can run for longer distances; faster; can smell, scent and track better; have specialised hunting skills for example the retriever; the pointer; the springer. One of the side-effects of domesticating the dog is that in behaviour terms it stays a juvenile all its life – it really is the Peter Pan of the animal world.

The first wolves to share our space in the world would have been the more confident type, overcoming natural shyness in order to get scraps of food. As they became bolder and ventured closer they would have started to trail our hunts, maybe even helping without realising it and so the tenuous bond been Canine and Primate would have been born. No-one knows if we invited the wolf in or the wolf invited himself but it's highly likely that it would have been a bit of both. As the wolf matured, any kind of behaviour that would have put the humans at risk wouldn't have been tolerated and no doubt the wolf would have ended up in the cooking pot, not just providing a high protein meal but valuable fat stores and warm pelts too. And so, without realising what they were doing at the time, those early humans were breeding for tameness which we now know brings with it many features like change in colour, a curly tail, floppy ears and a juvenile disposition.

Regardless of whether the dog is young or old, however, the bottom line is that the dog's brain is still 'hard wired' to pack mentality and a hierarchical social structure and we owe it to our best friend to learn how to make life easier and more relaxed for them living in the alien environment we call home. Also keep in mind that man too is a social creature who likes routines, rules and structures to follow – this is why the two species can live together in harmony, each giving the other what it needs to live a balanced life.

In the domesticated dog the basic instincts for pack behaviour are still very much in evidence. Males will compete with other intact males for the right to reproduce, even when females are not present. Intact females will also compete for their place, as the dominant female is the one that would, in the wild, be the first to breed with the dominant male. Neutering and spaying domestic dogs reduces this need to prove dominance for breeding purposes and can eliminate most, but not all, of the competition and fighting for this issue. The timing has to be right however to avoid health and behaviour problems as the dog matures.

By clearly understanding the pack issues and hierarchy system that dogs instinctively use, you can more clearly understand the behaviours that dogs use towards each other. This can be a great help not only during training of the dog but also to help keep his life as stress free as possible. Like with ourselves, stress can have many negative effects on health and demeanour, so reducing your dogs stress levels promotes an environment where he can be healthy and happy.

So how can we take advantage of this pack mentality? Well, as said earlier the dog is used to having a hierarchical structure where there is a leader and a follower, if you're not one you must be the other. This is just how it is with pack animals. Dogs cannot think like humans and therefore cannot be leader of our combined pack of humans and dogs; to ask it to do so would cause it stress and be unfair.

It is therefore our responsibility to establish ourselves in a position of authority and trust. If we fail to do this, then the dog may question our requests and authority. Many people assume that they are automatically the lead figure just because they are humans; at the end of the lead or 'own' the dog; they're not.

Like many things in life
you have to earn the right to be in a position of authority.

Being the leader does not mean you have to be big and aggressive. Nor does it mean that there has to be a battle of strength or wills, after which you emerge the victor. Anyone can be the leader and everyone in the household should be. It is an attitude: an air of authority. It is the basis for mutual respect, and provides the building blocks of communication between you and your dog. It never means being hard on your dog or displaying overt aggression. Think calm, confident, consistent, authoritative and affable and you will not go far wrong.

Isn't all this hierarchy stuff a bit confusing?
Absolutely not - personally, I tend to think of a dog or wolf pack like an 'old fashioned family' (which doesn't mean that I think of them as humans in fur coats... I view them very much as a different species but with a similar hierarchical structure to family life as our own).

Mum and Dad were in charge, made the rules and enforced them when necessary. There was a time for play and a time for calm. Dad generally had 'his chair' and although the kids were allowed to sit in it when he was at work, when dad came home they moved. This old fashioned family were good mannered, never dreamed of barging past elders to get through doorways first – in fact they would have been disciplined for not standing back and holding the door open. They didn't hassle visitors that came to the house, they generally said hello then disappeared, knowing that there would be rewards left from the visitors for being so polite or praise and a special treat later from parents. They gave to others before they had themselves (like sharing sweeties) and waited until they were told they could eat before they demolished the sarnies in the middle of the table – to do otherwise would have caused a stinging sensation on the back of the hand as, quicker than lightning, mum's resounding slap would have got there first.

Good behaviour outside of the home was something that was a general rule, not an exception. Children knew that they had to behave outside and woe betide if they forgot their P's & Q's. They knew that they couldn't be demanding in shops, lifting things off shelves or whining for food yet unpaid for. When they were little they were taught to walk politely with you, never tugging on your arm to get somewhere quickly or those nag, nag, nagging pulls on your jacket as you spoke to a neighbour. They were taught self-control.

A healthy adult would never dream of sitting while an old person or pregnant woman stood up on a bus or a train and a child would be the first to be squished onto an already loaded knee or made to stand to one side. Is this all sounding familiar?

For a good example of a pack leader you need look no further than your own school days. Remember the teacher that made you sit up in class, pay attention, do well for and get all your homework in on time... they may not even have been your favourite teacher. You knew however, that this was a teacher that could not be messed with. They probably never shouted and were highly unlikely to even raise their voice, you knew though, that beneath that kindly exterior there was a rod of steel. They were approachable, listened to you, reassured you when you were uncertain, cheered on your achievements and would defend you against others... they would also be the first to tell you to 'pull your socks up'; 'get on with it' or 'knock it off', swiftly followed up by a little smile and a nod no doubt.

Compare this then to a pack...

A pack is made up of an alpha male and alpha female, the dominant pair, the breeding pair, mum and dad if you like. You then have the next in command, the beta animal.

The beta is the bodyguard who, is not only sent out ahead of the pack to scout around, is generally the rank that doles out the discipline. Think of it as middle management; always having an eye on the job title above and having to deal with the 'un-pleasantries in the office' or of the young adult that's there supporting mum and dad ready to step in if help is needed with younger siblings or to take over the running of the household if need be. You then have the middle ranks; the brothers and sisters caught up in their own little world doing their own thing and being quite selfish about it in, for the majority of the time, an inoffensive way. And then finally, we have the omega rank. This is the rank that we want our pet dog to have.

Not out of bullying it and keeping it down and in its place as happens in the wolf pack - but because it is generally the softest, most easy going member of the pack and is the natural mediator, stepping in if excitement gets too high with a nudge and a lick. They are the rank designed to 'take the flak' if the pack is having a bad day and are generally the one that is turned to for a game of something or another. This rank very, very rarely makes a challenge for leadership and is generally accepting of its place in the order of things. In the large human family it would generally correspond to the happy go lucky, easy going, middle born brother that everyone turns to for off loading 'stuff', support and laughter.

In many ways that's what a pack is, a large family. Generally it's brothers and sisters, occasionally an aunt or uncle and sometimes an outsider, however, unlike an extended human family (for example daughter living at home with partner or as a single mum with young child) there can be only one breeding pair, and in fact, the females won't come into season while there is a strong alpha female.

So here we have alpha male and female doing what comes naturally... along come pups (or cubs if it's a wolf pack you've got in your mind while reading this).

Alpha female has already made a birthing den which will be a space that is just big enough for her and pups. Once she's given birth she'll only leave the den to go to the toilet and collect the food that the rest of the pack regurgitates for her. As the pups get older she'll leave them for longer periods and assign a 'nanny' who'll look after them while she's out hunting. As alpha female she's probably one of the best hunters and will need to resume hunting duties quickly.

The nanny can be either male or female and can be any of the middle ranks – chances are alpha female started 'training' them up when she became pregnant or they may be experienced nannies from previous litters, either way, she trusts them to apply the discipline and affection required in her absence.

So, as we were saying, alpha male and female do what comes naturally and along come the pups. The pups are born with a sense of smell and a sense of touch on the head and neck area only. The sense of smell is phenomenal - a dog has 220 million scent receptors in its nose compared to our 5 million, and they're all fired up and working at birth ! If any one thing can reinforce to us that the dog is a different species it's the sense of smell – we can't begin to comprehend what it must be like to smell not only stuff that's there now but also things from the past and to be able to differentiate between them... for us humans seeing is believing; for the canid however, if it can't smell it it doesn't exist.

It takes a couple of weeks for the touch sensation to be working 100%, about the same time that the eyes/ears open. In those first couple of weeks they are totally dependent on mum – they can't even toilet without stimulation as the sphincter reflexes aren't developed. They are born to strong but soft energy; however, mum doesn't need to be aggressive or throw her weight around to get the pups to do as they're asked. All it takes at a young age is a paw to pin them down or a nose to flip them over.

As they get older and their teeth come through so mum will leave them more and at around 3-4 weeks will start regurgitating food for them (it's around this time that breeders will start to introduce 'mush' into the diet). Nanny takes over more and more, guiding them gently through the maze of being a young pup in a pack. Puppies can however, do just about anything and the rest of the pack will humour them, letting them swing on their tails, ears, jump all over their backs and so on. They also have food regurgitated for them on command by all the other pack members; all the young pup has to do is lick lick lick at their mouths and out comes a warm and tasty snack.

There then comes a day – usually at around 4-4 ½ months old, when the pack decide that the puppy isn't a puppy any more, it's a young dog and it's time for it to grow up. And grow up it will.

Gone are the days of snacks on demand from all but the lowest ranking members of the pack. The young juvenile dog now runs the risk of getting its muzzle clamped, nipped or pinned for breaking the pack rules, regardless of how minor the indiscretion may be – whether it's grabbing a tail, looking at an important dog the wrong way, invading another's body space or cutting across the front of a senior ranking dog (you could think of this as a child barging past an adult to get through a door first – not a good idea, the primate in us would probably grab the child by the arm and bring them back – the canid would do something similar but with its teeth).

Discipline is applied calmly and swiftly: without aggression or repercussion.

The young dog will go rushing off on its own and try and figure out what happened. Eventually the dog **learns** that if it does that, that and that then its world turns to pants, however if it does that, then it gets left alone. And so the young dog **learns**, by its own means if you like, what's acceptable and unacceptable behaviour for the pack.

There's no shouting or aggression, just straight forward, easy to understand discipline. It's a case of this is how it is – fit in or get reprimanded. No normal dog wants that, after all they are a pack animal, so they learn how to behave and fit in.

They learn the boundaries of what's acceptable to their pack and what's not. There is no pack concept of positive reinforcement of acceptable behaviour, no treats for doing something right! The nuances of canine body language make it difficult for us to fully determine all the communication that goes on between dogs, but there are probably times when dogs let each other know that they are 'happy' with what is being done. Within the pack it is largely a case of learning by consequences for actions. In short, this paragraph is the kernel of all training; dogs learn through consequences.

Generally the pack will only really leave the den area (house & garden to the dog) to hunt, scent-mark and patrol their territory or to migrate. The whole pack, with the exception of the young and their nanny, will attend the hunt and, although only the adults are allowed to hold the responsible jobs of bringing an animal down/making the kill, a juvenile (sub-adult) may be allowed to join in on the chase.

Now, once the animal is down the alphas eat first (this is where the behaviour advice of eating before your dog comes from). It's not, as is often interpreted, alpha male, then alpha female, then second in command, third in command and so on. It's more a case of alpha male and female eat while the beta 'calms the troops' – they'll all have bloodlust going on for them. The beta will join the alpha and when they've had their fill will wander off and rest.

The remainder of the pack eat as a group, sometimes while beta and one alpha remains and sometimes not. They all have their 'piece' of meat as determined by their rank. A high ranking animal will have a good cut of meat, the low ranking a low cut, maybe the legs or tail. A lower ranking animal may 'challenge' a senior rank at this point in order to get a better cut of meat – it would never be done in reverse (rank is generally settled at playtime and then challenged while feeding).

This is one of the reasons why you put your dog's food down and leave him to it... to return could be interpreted as a challenge by a naturally senior ranking dog and can cause confusion in the dog.

No scent marking will be done at this time as to do so would jeopardise the success of the hunt and in turn the success of the pack. Scent marking is done during patrol but only by adult members of the pack and most frequently by the dominant pair. The alphas will choose which area will be marked and again the marking will take place according to rank with the lower ranks deferring to the more senior members. Sub-adult (juvenile) males only occasionally scent mark and sub-adult females never do, this is for a show of strength on behalf of the pack – a pack of 4 healthy adults is a stronger pack than 4 healthy adults and 6 juveniles... all those extra mouths to feed without the skill of the hunter.

The marking of the scent gives so much information to other packs, not just how many animals are in this particular territory but also the age of each animal, if the animal is healthy, what rank they hold (stress by-product) and, if it's up a tree, the size of the animal involved.

Whenever the pack leaves the den area it's always an ordered affair. It generally goes alphas, beta, middle ranks with the juveniles and then the omega. Graeme Norton managed to get some excellent footage of an Ethiopian wolf pack setting off on a hunt as part of the 'Saving Planet Earth' series (2007) – it was fantastic. Off they went single file, in rank order with about 3 metres between each wolf, all of them in that long rangy lope following in the paw prints of those that went before it.

The time when this may change is when migrating or while the pack is establishing itself in new territory when the alphas will send ahead the beta to scout the area and check for danger. If you ever get the chance to see Martin Clunes 'A Man and His Dogs' (2008) watch out for the African Painted Hunting Dogs – as they leave the enclosure for the first time, the collared 'alpha' goes second and the 'beta' crosses the doorway first... when it's been established that the coast is clear, the collared alpha moves back into the lead – absolutely classic.

After the animals have been out either hunting or reinforcing their territory markers, they return to the den for some time-out time. It can either be grooming, play or chilling out and sleeping. All of which are done within the hierarchical structure that forms a pack. The grooming is generally carried out by the alphas not only as a way of sharing affection but also a way to reinforce rank "I'm important enough to do this to you and touch you anywhere I want", normally ending with alpha holding or resting his head over the others withers/neck area.

Play can involve all members of the pack, but none more so than the juveniles which is a good way for them to practice hunting and stalking and working out where they're going to belong in the ranks – after all there's no point in trying to take on another for real if you can't even get him to move over in play!

Sleeping is done, and there is no other word for it other than, 'respectfully'. The alphas chose where they want to sleep and everyone else has to fit in around them. If it's a siesta then it's a less ordered affair than settling down for the night, where the alphas sleep surrounded by their pack, omega on the outside furthest away from alphas, however, in strange territory it may be the beta who's on the outside.

Living in a mixed species pack

The dog was the first domesticated animal, although whether we invited it in or whether it invited itself in is unclear. It is widely believed amongst scientists, and I too buy into this theory, that without dogs by our sides, allowing us to hunt more efficiently and watching our backs for danger, man wouldn't have been able to develop into the civilised beings that we are. Without the dog, it is doubted that we would have been able to settle in one place for any length of time and would have continued with the nomadic lifestyle.

The dog can, without doubt, read us better than any other animal on the planet, better even than our closest cousins the primates, as we share not only our hierarchical family structure with their ancestor the wolf, but also our social hunting instincts as well.

However much they can read us and however much we anthropomorphise them, they are still dogs, driven with different needs to us and we owe it to them to treat them how they need to be treated and not how we think they should be or even how we would like to be.

The canine...

Dogs are descendants of the wolf or wolf-like creature, its closest living cousin being the Grey Wolf. The wolf walks on all fours, has a relatively fixed thumb (dew claw) and can't communicate with the spoken language. In fact although wolves communicate through howling they very, very rarely bark – adult wolves never do, only the juveniles and then only occasionally (another indication that a dog is juvenile all its life!). When a wolf or a dog makes a lot of noise, it's generally calling the ranks to it for support. A dog that barks a lot is a dog that is viewed as weak – it's putting the pack in danger and won't be tolerated. Feral dogs and wild dogs generally don't bark... this is something that we've bred into the domestic dog either by accident or design.

When danger threatens, the pack (unlike the herd) will either run or stand and fight as a unit. An individual doesn't matter; the survival of the pack is the most important thing.

The strong silent type is generally the most senior rank in a pack. This is why dogs, generally, respond to the silent unassuming male in the human family – more of that in a minute. He's the dog that can bring the whole pack to attention with a look. He's affable, easy going, calm and relaxed but with a backbone of steel.

Dogs are constantly deferring to other dogs. They'll bow their heads, drop and soften their eyes, turn the other way, step back and lie down. Very respectful: when it's earned. Otherwise it's hard stares, heads up, tails up, barging, barging and barging some more and then ultimately the challenge.

Dogs have no morals or ethics whatsoever. It really is a "what's in it for me" approach to life. When the dog first comes across something it's generally "can I chew it?" "can I screw it?" "can I pee on it?" "what's in it for me?" It's a case of "what can I get away with and what can't I?"

Now that's not to say that your dog is plotting and scheming, just the opposite. The dog is reactive not proactive – he reacts in the moment to all that is going on around him, this moment. Now. This heartbeat. The previous heartbeat is in the past, the next in the future. The dog really is a very simple soul, living in the moment not worrying about tomorrow or the day after.

The primate...

Humans, as descendants of apes or an ape-like creature, walk upright as do apes most of the time (although if you watch teenage boys walking round with their mates you might doubt how upright we walk). It is believed that the speech area in the brain developed as a by-product of standing upright; combined with a shift in position and a stretching of the larynx as we became vertical beings made us able to communicate with complex sounds.

Primates (us and apes) get to the top of the pecking order by making noise. Think of the silverback male that pounds vigorously on his chest while the rest of the group gaze on admiringly. In captivity the senior ranking males have been known to settle rank disputes by banging metal lids together – the male that makes the most noise is the male that wins.

When danger threatens, the adults will protect the young every time. If all hope is lost then touching and re-assurance is the order or the day. A lot of the time when primates are scared they reach out and touch another primate or even another living breathing creature for reassurance – we're the only species type that will.

When we meet another person we communicate face on, eyeball to eyeball, hand outstretched in greeting, lips pulled back in a kind of grimace, generally with teeth on show. In fact, to do anything less is considered bad mannered and 'shifty'.

When we're giving approval to another person we'll give them a big grin, maybe a gentle punch on the arm or a couple of pats on the shoulder, if we know them well it may a hug, and we if really like them it'll be a big 'squishy' hug with a smacker on the cheek.

And so, in our supreme confidence we wander round making lots of noise, communicating in an eyeball to eyeball, chest to chest posture, yammering away 20 to the dozen and touching and patting everything we can get our hands on.... every inch a primate.

The mixed species pack

Although a lot of the time we tend to think of our dogs as humans in fur coats, (hopefully that way of thinking is on its way to being a thing of the past), dogs don't see us as bald upright dogs. They see us for what we are... another animal, a different species but still an animal nonetheless. This is our greatest advantage and is what we need to work on. It's a case of going to the lowest common denominator (remember those fractions!) and taking it from there.

In this case it's that we're both animals that know how to communicate with our bodies and our energy. So while your dog may be the highest ranking dog (especially if you have more than one) you are the highest ranking animal and therefore expect deference and self control from your pack members.

We need to learn to stop reacting like a primate and start reacting like a canine, because after all, not only are we the animal with the superior intelligence, but we're the ones who've removed the dog from its natural environment, domesticated it and made it totally dependent on us – we owe it this.

We need to remember that the pack is the be all and end all to the dog. The dog needs an authority figure it can trust to look after and ensure the survival of the pack. If the pack doesn't have a leader the pack will fail and this is not acceptable to the dog.

If you're not providing it, the dog, whether he wants to or not,
will assume the leadership role.

This is all very well if you have a dog that is a natural leader. They'll be easy going at home and try to control things outside, probably pull like a tank on the lead, stop to sniff and scent mark everything and have selective hearing on a recall.

If you have a naturally ranking 'beta' dog he'll probably throw his weight around at home pushing past, demanding attention, stealing stuff, probably pull like a tank on the lead, stop to sniff and scent mark everything and have selective hearing on a recall.

If you have a fearful dog or a dog lacking in confidence then you'll get a dog reacting out of fear and this is probably the worst – it'll more than likely try to control everything with aggression; after all that's the best form of defence. It'll be intolerant of visitors, worry about changes in the household routine and may become frantic when left. It may nip other dogs when out walking on the lead or launch a full scale attack... it may not pull on the lead or only pull when heading home. It may try 'herding' and nip you into keeping up.

None of these are nice places for your dog to be living in and are generally symptoms of a dog needing boundaries and a leader it can trust. Step up and be the leader your dog needs you to be so that he can relax and be 'just a dog'.

Does all this pack stuff still apply to domestic dogs?
Absolutely. Having a pack of 2 dogs I see it in action every day. In my canine pack my Labrador is more senior ranking. As such my Goldie will back away from the water bowl if my lab wants a drink. He'll wait quite patiently until the bowl is free – regardless of whether it's been emptied or not. If it's empty he'll either walk round looking for another bowl or wander off and wait for that one to be replenished.

When out and about walking he'll stand in line waiting for my lab to finish having a wee so he can wee on top of it. It can be quite funny really, here they are both bursting for the toilet and yet still following the canine code.

A couple of weeks ago I took my Goldie to visit a friends place. She has 7 working (gundogs) Labrador bitches, the alpha of which is my dog's sister. Well here they were all running down the dirt track when my Goldie went to run across the path of pack leader. He got a withering look which he immediately responded to and crouched down, belly almost on the ground as he curved around giving her a good 10 feet gap before he stood up and ran normally.

Putting it in action

Well the first thing we need to do is to work out what's acceptable to us and what's not. When we have boundaries in our pack, and reinforce them, the dog can relax because he knows what's expected of him and when. It also means that we don't have to constantly tell our dogs what they can and cannot do. They can mind their own p's and q's and get on with being a dog.

There are the usual rules that most people have heard of like, don't let your dog pull, don't let your dog sleep on your bed, eat before your dog and so on. What follows is a way you can live in harmony with your dog with minimal amount of conflict... in return you'll get a lifetime of deference – you just need to be consistent and persistent and insistent.

But first let's take a reality check and forget the myths...

"Everyone knows that to get a dogs attention you need to speak in a loud commanding voice". We now know that the louder you speak to your dog the less it will respect you… it's a canine not a primate. Dogs really do have excellent hearing so there really is no need to shout; all that noise will just mark you out as being unstable in your dog's mind.

"He knows that's my favourite table, he chewed it to get his own back 'cos I didn't have time to walk him this morning". He really doesn't and he really didn't. Chances are he had a bit of excess energy from missing his walk, maybe he was a bit bored, maybe he was a bit restless, maybe a bit anxious, the table smelled nice; tasted better; all that chewing released chemicals in his brain which made him feel better, relaxed him and helped him sleep. The 'Disney dog' that plots and schemes while you're out really doesn't exist – he can't, he simply hasn't got the brain power.

"Everyone knows that dogs are born loyal, trustworthy and want to please their owner" – actually dogs are like every other species on the planet; selfish, only interested in what's in it for them and ultimately the pack. Where do you think the saying "it's a dog eat dog world" came from? The wolves really didn't get together over

a Starbucks and say how about we give up our ways, all that freedom and doing what we like and instead become man's best friend and live only to please them and be at their beck and call.

"We all know that dogs love to be with their owners and that dogs want to go to them at all times". Well that's not strictly true either, dogs shouldn't come because they want to, they should think **they have to**. If they didn't, well, let me give you an example... Let's just say my dog was standing over there doing nothing and I called on him he'd go 'yay a bit of excitement' and come dashing over. If however, my dog was standing over there barking madly at a hedgehog and I called him, why would he want to come, 'I've got my excitement thank you very much – maybe I'll come later.'

One of the biggest secrets in the world of gundog trainers is that the dog actually has a choice whether it comes back or not. It's a secret that the dog should never find out...

For me, I believe dogs are capable of great love and great loyalty, the loyalty being more to a position in the pack than to an individual (new 'voted in' pack leader versus old pack leader), even though the love may still be there.

Put in place a leadership/lifestyle plan that you can follow for the rest of your life... Remember that as far as your dog is concerned, with rank comes privilege and while it may all seem small and petty to us humans, to a dog they can make the difference between comfort and struggle, health and sickness and ultimately life and death....

Discipline, praise and motivation

Hopefully you'll understand more about what goes on in a dogs head now that you've read the previous chapter. You'll understand why we have to have discipline when training a dog.

It's even more important when training a gundog. Why? Because for the most part, when your gundog is off the lead, he'll be working away from your side, either 10 feet or so quartering away putting up game, 30 feet away pointing at a target for you or 130 feet away picking up something to bring back. It is imperative therefore that when you say for example "stop", your dog stops immediately. The only way you can train this kind of response from your dog is through consequences for actions – both good consequences and bad consequences.

Let us just think about it for a minute.

- If we want a dog to repeat an action we reward him.
- If we want a dog not to repeat an action we discipline him.

Out of that comes motivation.

There are very few dogs that aren't food motivated and most are motivated by play. In the traditional world of the gundog, playing doesn't really happen as part of training and games of pull or tug are strictly forbidden. However, I tend to do both.

I've found that the only way to get a dog excited enough to teach self control away from a shoot is to play pull. There are lots of dangers in playing this game and I can't stress it enough that you never play pull with a dog that has no self control. The first thing you must do with your dog is teach him the Leave it! command (see training techniques) and then and only then do you embark on a game of tug and never with a dog that has shown aggressive tendencies.

When I play pull with my dogs, my gundogs, I always make a gurrrrr noise so that they know they're allowed to pull... no gurrrrr no pull, it's as simple as that.

Rewards and motivators

I encourage the use of food as a motivator when training new exercises, although never when training the retrieve... well not initially anyway. You'll see the use of food (dog 'sweeties'/dog treats/dog kibble, sausage, chicken or cheese) and toys in the training sections.

The ultimate motivator in training must be the handler/trainer/owner, which ideally will be the same person. **You are the motivating factor in your dog's life**. Dogs have been working with us and for us for years, for the most part for a nod or a "good dog" but occasionally for scraps.

If your dog does something you want to see repeated; smile, give him a scratch, a stroke, a sweetie, a play... anything to give him a warm and fuzzy moment. My lab will do anything for a good back scratch, my goldie prefers a firm neck massage – work out what does it for your dog and exploit it!

If you choose to use food don't rely on it. If every time your dog does what you want you give him food what will he do the first time you don't have any food treats with you. If you've got a bolshie dog you could end up with him snapping or barking at you in a typical "terrible two's tantrum"... "where's my treat, I want it now". Sounds a bit over the top but it's a well known response in the behaviour world. If you use food use it first to show what you want, then as a reward and then as a distraction; more on distraction later.

Remember the power of a smile when training your dog. From a very early age the puppy learns that great things happen around the person that is smiling, a cuddle, a scratch, food, a play; think back to all the times you've smiled at your puppy although you may not do it quite so much when they're an adult dog. Whenever your gundog is doing what you want him to do, especially in training, *smile*, get into the habit of it now and it will make your training at distance a lot easier.

Try to be conscious of your facial expression when training your dog, especially when you first start and it's all very new to you as well. We humans tend to frown when we're concentrating on something, more so when we're finding it difficult. This can give our dogs mixed messages... all this frowning when they're trying their best *and* getting it right. Do your dog a favour; *smile*.

Your voice is one of the most powerful motivators you'll ever have; it will also be your first method of discipline.

To motivate your dog with your voice use a high, excitable voice with rapid words, to praise use a calm, friendly and soothing voice and to reprimand or discipline use an unfriendly voice that is sharp and authoritative; remember also to use facial expressions at the same time. As detailed earlier dogs have very good hearing so there is no need to shout at them, even when disciplining; shouting is getting in touch with your inner-primate, but that does not translate into 'canine' very well so you can end up confusing your dog. Try to remain calm but use a deeper voice and be sharp with your commands.

Touch is also a wonderful and powerful tool. Don't give it away willy-nilly, make your dog earn it. Dog trainers and especially gundog trainers, will often tell their students to stop touching (and talking to) their dog – it's not because they're hard and they don't love their dogs... it's because they know the value of the touch and they want their dogs to work for it. Just imagine the absolute mayhem on a shooting field if every dog worked to the clicker or only for food... no, that's not for the working gundog – after a good day's work there's a stroke, a smile and a good rub down. To get to this stage however we need to reward the dog so that he understands what's required and what pleases us... lots of touching as a reward, food, toys, play – he'll get the idea quickly enough.

Training with food rewards and toys make the next bit easier which is distraction training. Whatever you use as a reward or a motivator becomes your distraction once your dog has learned self-control. For example when I first introduced food training with my Labrador all I had to do was go near a pocket and he'd spit the dummy out. Now he will hold the dummy while having a piece of food balanced on top of his head or his paws... self control induced by consistent training, praise and discipline.

Discipline

One of the first things we teach our puppies is NO – make the most of it, if it looks as if your dog is going to break a stay for example, use "no" followed immediately with a "sit" or "down" then "stay". To start off with you are guiding your dog through what you want, the "noo-o" then becomes a "NO!" or "AHHHHH!"

Play with your voice during training and see what works best for your dog both for motivation and discipline.

Don't think that discipline is a bad thing. It isn't. Dogs need boundaries and they need rules but more importantly, dogs need to know that if a rule is broken or a boundary is crossed there will be consequences.

I don't mean hitting your dog or doing the relatively common thing of the old style gundog trainer and taking your dog by the scruff of his neck and giving him a damn good shake (scruffing/scragging) or picking him up by his cheeks, lifting him to eye level and giving him a good shake whilst glaring at him and then throwing him down... discipline and harsh handling are worlds apart.

Training styles were very different 20 years ago, for example spaniels weren't made to walk to heel and were encouraged to hunt and go do their own thing until they were about 8-10 months old and were then brought in to heel in no uncertain terms. That's not to get on the proverbial 'high horse', that's just how it was then and it got results. However times have changed and obedience and control are taught as a pre-cursor to everything else.

> In my eyes there is no longer a place in dog training for this,
> discipline yes; harsh handling no.

The way that I discipline a dog is by making him do as he's told first time every time. Let's just say for example, you told your dog to sit and stay and he got up (assume this is a trained dog and you couldn't prevent him getting up with your voice), the first time he broke the stay I would escort him back to the mark, firmly but gently by the collar, set him up for the stay and repeat the command.

For repeated offences I would combine the scruff and the collar and, for a dog that was taking 'liberties' (or to use my favourite training phrase "dicking about"), I would frog march him back in no uncertain terms using the scruff of his neck with a scowl upon my face – no words. Once upon the mark it would be a firm "stay". After 5 paces I would return to the dog and praise him for staying and call it a day with that exercise, have a play and a bit of fun.

This communicates to the dog that I mean what I say but that I'm also a fair and firm leader, indulging in play once the dog has acquiesced to my wishes.

If the dog is at distance and starts to 'dick about' then generally a low growling AHHHHH will work wonders at pulling your dog up short, you can then call them in your normal voice or give them another command. Why the low growling? Well growling is a signal that dogs give to other animals which means back off, continue doing what you're doing and it's going to end badly for you. The bigger the dog the lower the sound they tend to make. So, by growling AHHHH in a very low voice you're communicating to your dog that you mean business and you're too big to mess with. The main thing is not to overdo it and if you do AHHHHH your dog, be prepared to follow it up immediately with a consequence if your dog doesn't respond...

One of the Labradors that was training with me started to push her owner, you may have experienced it yourself, dog dancing around with the dummy, running past the owner trying to incite a game of chase, this dog also had a bit of an aggressive streak so it was important to deal with it immediately. As the dog ran past the owner I growled, the dog stopped looked at me and decided I wasn't a threat – as she went to run away again I charged! Ran straight at her with a furrowed brow, as soon as she backed off I took the pressure off her and had her owner call her in. She didn't do it again. You have to bluff with your dog; you know you'll never catch them but they don't have to know it as well (in fact they should never know you can't catch them!); you know you'd never rip their throats out but they don't have to... bluff. While I can't say "works every time" it certainly works enough to add it to a book.

Manners Not Mayhem:
how to avoid having a pushy gundog

I remember years ago meeting Noel Hutchinson for the first time, he was the only non-food trainer of competition obedience dogs in New Zealand. On meeting my lab his first comment was "your dog has atrocious manners"... I was speechless. I had a well trained gundog! He was right of course; my lab could have been the best trained gundog in the world but his manners left a lot to be desired... at home we called him Bargy Bart. Not for long... within a few days he was well trained and well mannered.

So how do we go about having a well mannered dog at home. Simple really, like with children, we need to work out some rules at home that they understand. As you'll have read by now, dogs have an innate set of rules that they must follow however they can be summed up, quite succinctly into one.

Show deference at all times to a senior rank

However, this can be a bit misleading and confusing for pet dog owners and so, as a behaviourist (along with other successful behaviourists) I give clients a plan to follow that shows ways to make their dog appreciate and follow the one rule above. They're based on common sense and are very easy to follow.

The most important thing however is to be consistent.

Dogs, with their "what's in it for me attitude", will exploit and manipulate you if you're not. If there's a one in 10 chance that he'll be allowed on the sofa then he'll persist until he's up there and you're on the floor; if there's absolutely no chance of him being allowed up he'll stop trying.

I find that too often owners will read a book saying do this or do that and your dog will respect you, however, a lot of the time the 'do this' and 'do that' are training techniques designed for you to control your dog rather than behavioural techniques designed for your dog to control himself. In this busy world there are times when we have to leave our dogs alone and this should not be a cause for concern; rather the dog should be able to exert self control and keep himself in check.

The difference between training and behaviour

For me the biggest difference between training and behaviour is that with training you control your dog through a command for example, sit, down, come, stay etc., with behaviour you teach your dog self control generally using your body or props and are more often than not silent; you tend to get inside of your dogs head and think about how other dogs would respond in that situation for example barging and body blocking, and then you respond accordingly.

Most of the time however, you would use training to change the behaviour that you don't want into the behaviour that do want, for example walking nicely on the lead.

This chapter is focussed on behaviour and the next two on training.

Doors and doorways

Doors and doorways are so important to dogs. Why? Because generally something really exciting happens on the other side of it and the dog wants to be part of it and get there first so as not to miss out.

You must have seen, either in the movies, cartoons or even with your own dogs where the dogs scramble to squeeze out of the door ahead of everyone else that they quite literally turn into the cartoon dog running on the polished floor.

After a period of time of putting up with the barging and the scrambling some clients decide enough is enough and tell their dog to sit and wait. This leads to an explosion of energy when the dog is released – the owners of course think that their dog is showing them respect by them 'making him wait'. Take it from me he's not.

The owner is controlling him with the trained sit stay/sit wait. The dog hasn't learned self control and if the owner forgets to tell the dog to wait the dog will still barge past. The technique that follows is one that is used again and again by successful dog behaviourists to teach owners how to gain respect and self control from their dog. First of all though, why bother? Surely the dog getting out of the door first isn't such a big deal. To a human, perhaps not: to a dog, most definitely yes. In the dog world it's all about getting there first, through the door first, to the food first, to the garden first, to the ball first and so on.

If you're a man reading this you'll understand this as its fits very much with the male psyche of competition whereas a woman's psyche is all about co-operation. If you've ever been to see "Defending the Caveman" with Mark Little based on John Gray's work, you'll recognise the scene where the men are round a mates house watching footie and they run out of chips. Immediately there's a competition with one man saying "out of chips", another "I brought the chips", followed by "I put the chips in the bowl", followed by "I watched you put the chips in the bowl"... and so on until the man who can't 'compete' has to go refill the bowl. This is compared with a group of women having a girls night in and the chips run out with one girl saying "out of chips" and all of them getting up en-masse heading to the kitchen and helping each other to replenish the bowl of chips, generally including topping up wine glasses and clearing up. Competition versus co-operation. The last time me and my husband went to see it (I've seen it three times now) I thought "you know he could be talking about a dog". If you haven't seen this one man play keep an eye out for it.

Okay back to doorways. The other reason not to let your dog go first, purely and simply is safety. You have no idea what is on the other side of the door (unless of course it's glass) and a lot of times doors lead to roads. You would never let a child run through a door ahead of you without first checking it's safe for them to do so, the same should apply to your dog.

Another reason is that if your dog always takes a step back and allows you to go first, which he will if you follow the technique below correctly, is that you don't have to worry about carrying hot things around your dog and doorways. A couple of weeks ago I was padding around in my dressing gown and made myself a cup of soup. Carrying it into the sitting room my dressing gown sleeve caught on the door handle and I ended up tipping scalding hot soup all over the floor directly in front of me to the left. Had my dogs not have taken a step back and let me go first then I have absolutely no doubt in my mind that they would have gotten the soup over their heads.

Like most behavioural techniques this is about self control. That is the dog controlling himself not us controlling him.

Leaving and entering together
First of all put your dogs lead on, this will give you control if it all goes 'pear-shaped'.

As you approach the doorway make sure the lead is loose and has no tension going down it to your dog. Open the door ever so slightly and as your dog goes to go through, close it quickly. Do this a few times opening it a bit more each time and every time your dog tries to go through shut the door in his face. Although you have to shut the door fast in order to make your dog back off (which is what this exercise is all about), the aim is not to catch your dog with the door, hence opening it only slightly to start off with. If however, you do catch your dog put it down to experience and work on improving your timing.

Once you can get the door open start to go through it without your dog. If your dog starts to move forward then step into the space where your dog is heading (body blocking or herding, see below) and claim the space; this is another example of communicating in 'canine' rather than primate.

When your dog backs off you can walk through the door and call your dog through from the other side.

It is so important that you do not give a command at all during this exercise and much better to do the whole thing in silence, from putting the lead on to calling your dog through.

Letting your dog go first
There are times when you want your dog to go first, or even go through the doorway without you, letting your dog out into the garden for example. In these instances all you do is set it up as we have above right up to the point where you start to go through the door. Instead step to the side, turning sideways as you do so and with a sweeping movement with your arm closest to the door say "in" or possibly "out" or "through" or "off you go" (if it's into the garden) or any other command you decide to use.

The main thing is that unless you send your dog ahead of you then you go first.

Letting your dog into the room with you
This is when you're in one room and your dog is in the other. You may want him to join you or you may want to join him, regardless of which way round it is your dog must step back and let you decide what's happening next.

Open the door just a crack so you can, if possible, see your dog. Close the door with a resounding snap. Open the door a little bit wider and close the door again. Open it a little bit wider still being prepared to close it quickly should your dog start to move forward. Keep repeating this exercise until you can stand with the door wide open without your dog trying to barge through. Then quite simply walk through the door or call your dog in to join you.

You can also use this technique for releasing your dog from its crate or dog carrier in the car so that he learns not to barge past you to get out, rather to wait politely until given permission.

Doing things silently with dogs, as you may have guessed by now, really is talking their language.

If you have the type of door that has a lip or skirt on the bottom (outside doors, French doors etc.,) I cannot stress enough to watch for your dog's paws with this exercise. If need be practice with other doors in the home until your dog understands he's supposed to back off and then use this doorway. Please, please, please be extra careful with this type of door.

Body Blocking/Herding

I tend to use blocking to mean when I'm standing still or moving my body weight from side to side to block a dogs access to something and herding to mean, well herding... It's much easier to describe.

Say for example two dogs were heading for the same space, maybe a doorway, one of two things could happen; one dog could step back and let the other dog through or one dog would barge (either using shoulder or hip) the other out of the way. In the latter instance, neither dog would have his 'feelings hurt' but he would know to show deference next time at the doorway.

This is what you try to emulate when you block your dog at the doorway. So, you've done the opening and closing of the door and you start to walk through the doorway. As you do your dog tries to side step you (and why not, he has gotten used to barging past you and have you defer to him!) step into the space that your dog is trying to squeeze through – your dog will jump back out of your way. He may try going round to the other side, repeat the process so that you're blocking your dog from going past. Make sure you step into the space and not use your leg as a hook which is a classic primate response... I can't use my hands to pull my dog back so I'll use my leg as an arm instead. Don't just stick your leg out either... you are trying to emulate the dogs innate behaviour in a two legged upright way which means claiming the space by moving into the place where the dog is trying to get to.

Herding I tend to use to make the dog do something without actually touching the dog. Think for a minute of a sheepdog herding sheep. If the dog wants the sheep to go to the left, he doesn't stand to the left of them going "here sheepies, here sheepies, have some nice sweeties" he heads to the right of them and using his energy/presence pushes them forwards so that they turn to the left. If they try to break the dog rushes around them and pushes them forward in the direction he wants them to go in. The dog is controlling the space around the flock rather than the flock itself.

That's what you need to do with your dog. Let's just say you want your dog to go on his bed. You've taught him the command but sometimes it takes 4 or 5 times of you saying "Fido on your bed" for your dog to actually do it. Instead of teaching your dog to ignore you (which is what you'd be doing if you kept repeating the command) tell your dog to go on his bed. If he doesn't do it first time then stand up and walk past him so that he's between you and the bed. Point to the bed (we'll get to pointing later) and walk towards your dog, saying "in your bed". Be the sheepdog herding the sheep – if he tries to go one way control the space, be relentless and be serious. The look on your dogs face will probably make you want to laugh as all of a sudden you're talking his language, however this is the worst thing you can do as you'll communicate to your dog that you're not being serious. Instead wait until he's on his bed before you release your laughter.

Herding is such a great tool to use with dogs, they understand what you're doing and respond. You can use it to bring your dog in from the garden (providing you've got a normal size garden and not a field), just position yourself so that your dog is between you and the door, point and say "in" as you herd your dog in through the door.

I can't stress enough though to keep in mind that you're getting in touch with your 'animal' self rather than 'human with a quirky sense of humour' self and so you need to be serious and in a serious frame of mind while herding otherwise your dog will pick up on the joke and before you know it you'll have incited that favourite of all canine games.... chase!

Feeding time

This aspect of leadership seems to draw a mixed reaction; some say it's a waste of time, others say it's cruel and yet others say it causes begging. Although I eat before my dogs it tends to depend on what I'm doing that day as to who eats when, I do not, however, stand by their food bowl and pretend to eat from it.

My routine is to walk the dogs first thing, feed them when their breathing has settled, leave them in the garage for an hour or so to dry off and chill out. Bring them in the house, generally after I've sorted myself out for the morning. Lunchtime I eat in front of my dogs – they don't have lunch. When we (my family) eat the dogs know that they're to go on their beds; they do so and go to sleep until something more interesting happens. Tea time I walk my dogs and if they're wet they go back in the garage, if not they come in and get fed. We eat later about 7:30… so sometimes I eat before my dogs and sometimes I eat after but when I'm eating my dogs are on their beds, end of story.

Some people seem to think that eating in front of your dog will cause begging behaviour. Absolutely not. The only thing that will cause begging behaviour is feeding your dog from your plate or tearing a bit off your sandwich and giving it to him. When you've done it once your dog will look again and again; they can be very, very persistent. Then you'll find you won't be able to resist their big brown eyes and before you know it you've got an established begging behaviour.

> Begging is nothing to do with eating in front of your dog and
> everything to do with feeding him 'from your plate'

Putting down the food bowl

Some *people* make their dogs sit and wait until released and some *dogs* make themselves sit and wait until released. From a young age I've established that my dogs touch nothing unless I say so whether that's a food bowl going down or food dropped by accident or design.

It means I can leave a sandwich on a plate on the settee go out of the room and know it is safe… no permission, no food. How do you achieve it? The same way we instil all good behaviour in dogs, calmly, consistently and silently.

Prepare your dog's dinner as usual. Say nothing to your dog and put the bowl down in front of him. If he moves towards it pick it up… he'll look at you with a goofy look on his face – wait until he sits (and he will). Repeat the exercise; put the bowl down if your dog goes to move pick it up. Keep doing it until he doesn't attempt to get up from the sit then release him with your usual "okay" command. It won't take long. Over time you can slowly draw out the length of time you leave him waiting, perhaps moving away from the bowl before you do so.

Another take on the above is to put the bowl closer to you than to your dog and as you release your dog slide the bowl towards him with your foot.

Leaving your dog to eat

Like every single aspect of dog ownership there are people who say leave your dog alone to get on with it and others that say you should be putting your hand in your dogs bowl or lifting it up and away from them. There are pluses and minuses for both.

When your dog is very young I suggest adding food to your dog's bowl as he is eating so that he always associates good things happening when you approach the bowl. Sometimes putting down a half portion and tipping more food in as the young dog is eating or lifting it up just as your dog finishes and adding more. If I have kitchen scraps I may add some to the bowl, regardless of whether it's full or empty, but making sure that the dog sees me bringing more food.

For the most part however, I leave my dog to enjoy his meal. From a dog's perspective only a low rank would approach another dog while he's eating to 'beg' for scraps or alternatively to make a challenge for the food. A senior rank would never do that... why challenge a lower ranking dog for his lower quality cut of meat? Also a senior rank would only have to look or stare in the direction of the food and the lower rank would walk away from it. A good example would be to look at my two dogs. If my Goldie finishes first, and he generally does, he'll skirt around the Labrador showing respect, he would never walk directly up to the food bowl as that would be a challenge and he could get hurt. Likewise with the water bowl; if my Labrador is drinking my Goldie would never approach, he waits in the wings until my Lab has had his fill – if he's drinking and my lab started heading directly towards it then he will back away showing deference and will stand about 8 foot away until the Labrador has finished.

You may have noticed that the key with dogs is an indirect approach as opposed to direct approach: a direct approach is a challenge or can be construed as one whereas an indirect approach is a mark of deference.

Furniture

This can be a real dilemma... for some people it's "absolutely" whilst others think "why on earth do you want a smelly hairy dog on your sofa?"

Part of the problem is that to ensure you get good behaviour from your dog you have to be absolutely consistent. Many times I've visited clients that allow their dogs on the sofa and I've asked "Is the dog always allowed up?" "oh yes" is the general reply. This is met with "always, even when he's wet or smelling of fox pooh?" to which the answer is always "oh no".

Unfortunately, the dog doesn't know he's wet or smelly; all he knows is that the head of the house is inconsistent to say the least, sometimes allowed up, other times shouted at to get down. A dog needs a stable leader and someone who is inconsistent is, in the dogs mind unstable and therefore shouldn't be calling the shots. This is when the dog can start to take things into his own paws (so to speak) and start to ignore commands, or worse, decide he's staying on the settee and get his weapons out when you try to get him down.

I don't want my dogs on the sofa after they've had a good roll so I don't let them up, however, if you want your dog on the settee with you set the rule that it's by invite only and if he gets up without being asked shove him off; remember that shoving, not shouting, is how to communicate in 'canine', or rather 'touching' as shoving has connotations of aggression and it is a matter of pushing your dog gently but firmly off the furniture rather than the primate reaction of a big shove to unbalance someone and knock them to the ground.

The other part of the problem is that dogs have no concept of equality; ownership yes, equality no. When your dog is on the settee uninvited, with or without you, then as far as the dogs is concerned the settee belongs to him... how can it be any other way as in the simple unreasoning mind that belongs to the dog "I'm on it therefore it's mine". This applies to anything really, your settee, your lap, your bed.

The bed however is also a very, very high value resource to the dog. Not only is it where your scent is strongest but in a pack only the most important members are allowed to sleep near pack leader. By allowing your dog on your bed you are seriously raising his status. And if he's an intact male then aggression may well follow... imagine the following scenario but from a dog's point of view.

Here he is on the bed with the two most important family members, 'alpha male and alpha female' for want of a better term. Alpha male gets up to go to the toilet... dog spreads out, right out, probably into the space that the man has just left. He goes to get back in and the dog won't move – why should he the bed now contains an alpha male and an alpha female? The man grabs the dog while glowering at him, dog reads a challenge and responds accordingly. A few things can happen next. With a small dog sometimes the female will cuddle and reassure the dog that it's just "daddy" getting back into bed, very effectively providing positive reinforcement to attack whenever "daddy" goes to get into bed; the man can raise the stakes by being firmer or aggressive and the dog backs off and gets off the bed OR the man can raise the stakes by being firmer or aggressive and the dog attacks.

Regardless of what the response is the dog has had his status raised and the next time the behaviour will become learned and will escalate... much better not to put yourself or your dog in the situation in the first place and keep the dog off the bed and out of the bedroom.

To ignore or not to ignore

Do you ignore your dog when you get in from work or doing the shopping because you've been told that that's the thing to do to gain respect? Do you know why you're doing it and more importantly has it worked?

"The Ignore" is a technique that takes a lot of practice and a lot of discipline; not from the dog from us. Just run this scene through in your mind; 2 dogs which know each other well and are, for want of a better word, friends. They see each other from across the field and one runs towards the other head down and tail wagging so hard that the whole body moves with it, he may be crouching down and trying to get to the side of the other dogs jaw to lick at it. What's the other dog doing? He's ignoring him. Head up, tail up, eyes front, body proud he allows the 'subservient' dog to pay homage; he may even walk a few strides as if there was nothing there. If the subservient dog's lickiness gets too much he will tip his nose up and look away.

That is "The Ignore".

What the subservient dog is doing is approaching in an indirect manner (not a threat); crouching to display a lower status and to get lower, physically as well as psychologically; licking at the face is a juvenile display of affection – he is saying to the senior rank I'm low ranking, a juvenile, a puppy, look after me. When returning from a hunt a wolf may regurgitate his lunch under such lavish displays of neediness; luckily this is something we've managed to breed out of the domesticated dog.

To recreate it in your home, what I advise clients (and you) is to take a breath just before they open the front door and focus on a task, normally walking to the kitchen and putting the kettle on or going to the toilet. The whole focus needs to be on the kettle and your eyes should be looking for it as soon as you open the door; at this moment in time your dog doesn't exist. Put the kettle on, go to the loo. Focus: kettle, toilet. Then back to the kitchen to make a cuppa. Focus: kettle; toilet; tea. By this time your dog should have calmed down a bit.

Congratulations you are now talking dog and you're not using any words or making any noise. It is a wonder that primates and canines ever managed to communicate in the first place; perhaps early man was more of the strong silent 'grunting' type!

At this point for me it's a dash to the bottom stair to indulge in a big scratch and tummy rub for my woofers. Remember the quickest way for your dog to show you deference around the home is to treat it as another dog would which is to ignore it, completely and utterly.

The routine in the morning when getting up is the same... go downstairs make yourself a cuppa and then say good morning to your dog. What you'll find is that it doesn't matter what clothes you're wearing or what you're carrying you can walk around the house without being mobbed.

Another time to use The Ignore other than when coming home is when you're eating. Those big brown eyes just boring into you, "look at me.... look at me". You look and the dog moves towards you; you talk to your dog "would you like some of this?"; you give your dog the remains of your sandwich and get on with whatever you were doing. No big deal right?

Well looking at it like that, no big deal. But what just happened from the dog's point of view?

Well he just did "the stare"; a soft stare rather than a hard glaring stare but a stare nonetheless. You responded to the pressure from your dog and gave him what he wanted... food. You've just communicated that not only if he stares he will get food, but also that he can control your behaviour just by staring at you: a sobering thought eh? Time to practise The Ignore, perhaps?

Time out

No doubt when you read the title you thought I was talking about giving the dog a 'time out' as you would with a naughty child. No not time out for the dog. Time out for me or time out for you.

Sometimes, regardless of how much I want my dogs to be with me, I just want a little bit of 'me' time... and if you feel the same, trust me, there's nothing wrong with that; it's just a bit like wanting to get away from the kids for a little while.

If you're still crate training then a good way of getting some time to yourself or 'dog free moments' is to just leave your dog in the crate for an hour whilst you go and do something else, that way you know your home and your dog are safe (especially important if your dog is young).

I've taught my dogs a command which is "not you!" It's surprisingly easy to teach and the majority of dogs get it straight away. Walk into a room with your dog beside you, as you cross the threshold reach down with your open hand in front of your dogs face and say "not you"; see the how to train it in the next section.

Trained For Life...

Before we get into the "how to train a..." we first of all need to understand how learning takes place. Because I actually want you to read about learning without falling asleep I've kept it short, simple and sweet; personally I think there's nothing worse than reading a book that teaches you new things but takes all your energy to stay awake long enough for it to make sense, so here we go... no matchsticks necessary.

How learning takes place

When we do something, nerve cells in the brain, known as neurons are fired up. They talk to each other in a way similar to passing a baton in a relay race, forming a pathway; a neural pathway. Just like passing the baton becomes quicker and more fluid with practice, so too the more an action is repeated the more established the pathway and the quicker and easier the action and reaction, until it eventually becomes an automatic learned response like driving a car or riding a bike for example.

The simplest way to remember the process is to think of it like a field of long grass. The first time you walk across the field may take a while and you'll bend the stalks. Next time you'll make more of an impression and so on. By the time you've walked the same path 20-30 times there'll be a bit of a track and you'll be able to walk it faster. Within a short space of time you'll have an established track that you'll use every time rather than walking across the 'untouched' area.

Now think of a learned behaviour in a dog; the easiest is chasing a cat as most dogs do so and you will either have seen it or experienced the reaction first hand... The first time the dog sees a cat whilst out on lead he may try to chase the cat a bit tentatively, maybe showing a bit of interest and pulling a little. However as the behaviour becomes more established so does the speed of the reaction - the dog may only be pulling as much as he ever did but the speed in which he reacts is much faster and as such becomes an out and out lunge... mix this with some of the chemicals that are flying around the brain and you could have a lunging barking snarling dog.

To change behaviour you need to do two things. Firstly stop/prevent the dog from using the neural pathway that has been set up. The way that I do it initially is to let the dog make the mistake and then correct it the first time, thereafter working on the intention of action or when the dog 'thinks' about chasing the cat; preventing him from going down the path in effect. Secondly, train the dog to do a new behaviour, for example walking with me on a loose lead when he sees a cat, in effect setting up a new neural pathway or dirt track across the field, if you like.

By catching the intention rather than waiting for the action you're stopping the old unwanted pathway being used... by doing this, just like a field reclaiming a track, the pathway in the brain will die out through lack of use. The saying "use it or lose it" springs to mind here.

This is why it's so important to repeat over and over again anything that is being learned in the same systematic way... it's also why behaviour that you don't want should be corrected rather ignored... we only want the neural pathway established for the behaviour we want, not the behaviour we don't want. A simple example is to think back to when you were learning to read. The alphabet was recited over and over again - if you pronounced a letter wrong you would have been corrected and made to repeat the letter with the correct pronunciation...

The same but different

Now imagine that the dirt track that you made across the field earlier is now covered with thick ice. The track is familiar but slippery and so you're being tentative walking under the new conditions – you need to call on more resources, more 'pathways', than normal to do a walk you're familiar with. This is what happens when you take a dog to a new place and ask him to do something that we think is familiar - because the conditions have changed the response to them is different.

This is why it's so important to repeat over and over again anything that is being learned in the same systematic way in various conditions.

Say for example you taught your dog to 'sit' on carpet... that would have fired up the touch sensors on your dogs pads in relation to the texture of the substance he's on. You'd then tell your dog to sit - the pathway (to overly simplify it) would be something like "sit".... on soft squidgy fluffy stuff yet firm but yielding, rifle through commands.... come, down, sit ... ah 'sit' got that one; fire up the body mechanics (muscles) to produce a sit.

If you then 'told' your dog to sit on wooden decking for example, he may not have made the association with the texture he was feeling in his pads with the body mechanics required for a sit and so may flounder. This is why we train on lots of surfaces and in lots of environments so that 'sit' appears in every pathway regardless of what stimuli is underfoot or around in the environment.

As we increase our dogs 'intelligence' through systematic learning they can make the leap from say wooden decking to polished wooden floors, tight weaved carpets to deep pile etc., and so we don't have to train the action, only give the command; a bit like when we first walk on frozen pavement and frozen dirt tracks... we have to learn to apply the same walking technique to both surfaces in order to be confident while walking on any frozen area.

Sorry were you talking to me?

A mistake that a lot of us make a lot of the time, myself included, is indulging in a constant stream of words to our dogs; things like "oh I think I'll make a cup of tea now" or "is that the time" or "it's getting dark already" or ... well you get the idea. Then, when the dog starts to respond we think that the dog understands what we're saying and before we know it we have a severe case of verbal diarrhoea whenever we're around the dog and, because they understand us so well, we anthropomorphise them at every turn.

"And why not?" I hear you ask. We have an animal that looks at us intelligently, doesn't answer back, responds accordingly (well according to us anyway) and is always there for physical contact.... oh did I say that they understand every word?

And now for the proper answer to "why not?" Well, by constantly talking to our dogs we're teaching them that our voice has no meaning and that they can 'zone out' to it; if we include the dogs name a lot we're teaching them to ignore their name also. Just imagine that you live with someone who walks around talking to them self or thinks out loud a lot, you'll learn very quickly that the words don't apply to you and so you stop hearing them. Welcome to the world of the dog.

If you want to have a conversation with your dog, a verbal monologue anyway, call your dog to you and then go for it – as far as your dog is concerned he will be getting praised for coming to you and then you'll both feel good.

"But my dog understands what I say, I know he does". Well, what you call understanding is basic conditioning, nothing more and nothing less. If you use the same words over and over again the dog will put them together with what comes next; a bit like training the 'sit', the dog associates words with an action however, they don't understand 'sit' to mean the whole range of 'sitting' past, present and future, in the way that we do.

Let me give you an example... somewhere down the line I started to say "right then" before I got up and did something; "right then, shall I feed you?" "right then, lets' go for a walk" "right then, cup of tea" it now evokes a response in my dogs that is instant – they can be sound asleep on their beds but when I say "right then" even quietly, I get the same effect as a sergeant major shouting "on your feet soldiers", the dogs are up and ready to move, even while they have blurry eyes and sleep lines.

Basic conditioning
It doesn't matter what words you use either, your dog really couldn't care less, providing you're consistent you'll be able to condition him to a verbal command.

As a bit of fun I trained both my dogs to get up and walk out of the room whenever someone said "ungawa", no doubt if you're of my generation you've just got a visual picture of Johnny Weissmuller standing in a clearing wearing a loincloth and turning the lions away with a grunted "ungawa". With conditioning any word really will do; it's being consistent that counts.

You don't need words to have a conversation with your dog. Dogs are masters at reading body language and facial expression; they have to be; they simply haven't got the brain power or the right equipment in their throats for verbal speech.

Human beings have two areas in their brains that allow verbal speech. Broca's area which is associated with the production of language, the spoken word and Wernicke's area which is associated with the processing of the words that we hear. Both areas are named after the scientists that discovered these functional areas of the left hemisphere. Without getting overly technical, these two areas are connected by a large bundle of nerve fibres resulting in the human production and understanding of speech; if any of these areas are damaged then the spoken word is affected, that's presuming of course that the larynx or voice box is working effectively.

Now, because we stand upright rather than on all fours, there is a 90 degree bend in the windpipe, the pharynx; the dog's windpipe has only a slight bend to it. It is this almost right angle bend in the throat that allows the voice box to be lengthened thereby making different pitches of sounds. We also have a rounder, larger tongue than a dog, whose is reasonably short and flat making it impossible to curve around into the necessary position for those complex vowel sounds.

Stanley Coren describes it beautifully in his book How to Speak Dog as "This is much like what happens with a toy balloon. If you blow it up and release the pressure on the opening, the air rushes out silently. Slightly stretching the rubber at the opening to make a narrow slit causes the outward rushing to make sounds, which will vary in pitch as you vary the tension."

It is believed, although not proven, that the transformation of the brain and larynx were bi-products or side effects if you like, of humans standing upright thereby separating us once again from the rest of the animal kingdom.

So hopefully you can now see that it's all down to consistent conditioning of a word tied in with an action; the reason why it is so important to work out what your commands are going to be and using them and only them... remember we can grasp the 'meaning' of the word sit and can apply it to different situations, including the past present and future whereas a dog needs to be conditioned to the situations it's used in before he gets it.

Never forget your dog is a predator... a hunter

Who wants to go hunting?

There is no such thing in a dog's mind that equates with 'going for a walk'. He goes hunting, territory checking and scent marking but he doesn't actually go for a walk because it's a nice day, the sun's shining and the birds are singing. The dog is very focused in this act as it means he gets to reinforce his territory, scent his area and meet others of the same species; this doesn't mean however that he gets to mob every dog he meets, rather he gets to smell them.

You may have seen dogs on your walk become bolshie or even aggressive over time with dogs that are met. Sometimes this can be because the dog is an important dog at home and is walked in the same place time and time again. The dog, because he's a dog, starts to view the walk as his 'territory' and, because he really is a very important dog, starts to decide who is and who is not allowed on it.

From the moment you think "time for a walk" or "need to walk the dog" you're acting with purpose and intention and the dog will pick up on it. As soon as your dog gets excited and starts to run back and forth he's trying to take control of the situation.

Take your time, lean against the wall, don't give in to your dog's bullying to hurry, hurry, hurry.

Tell your dog to 'sit' and put the lead on. If the dog jumps about etc., find somewhere you can tie the lead to and go and sit down. As the animal in charge of the home you're the animal that says when to hunt, what to hunt and in the manner of it; not your dog.

A really good place is the bottom of the stairs, on the banister if you have big dog or hooked over the radiator knob if you have a smaller breed. Take your time and take a breath.

When your dog is calm walk towards him and if he goes to get up back off. He should be sitting or lying calmly before you approach. The first few times you try this routine it will take a while as you're shifting the power centre back to yourself; remember this will pay dividends in having a dog that respects your actions. When you can pick up his lead with him sitting, (have faith, it will happen eventually) follow the doorway routine as detailed earlier and you're off, out of the den and on the hunt.

This is normally where it all goes pear shaped and the dog begins to pull. Before we go on to why a dog pulls and how to train him not to I want you to think of a time when your dog sat beside you and leaned against your leg. If you gently put your weight against the dog he would lean more – dogs are pressure animals which means that if they feel steady pressure they'll meet it.

Now think about a time when your dog leant against you and you slowly moved your leg away… did he fall over or stumble? Same thing, as you moved away the dog wanted to maintain the pressure and so tried moving with you to keep it there.

Back to lead walking; think about what you're doing with your dog by allowing the lead to go tight… yup you're meeting his pressure and encouraging him to pull. So here you are walking down the street with a tight lead and the dog meeting your pressure – or you're meeting your dog's pressure whichever way you want to look at it.

But firstly...

Left or Right?

I'm quite often asked whether our dogs should walk on the left or on the right or whether we should allow them to meander across us choosing which side to walk on themselves.

My reply? If you're right handed your dog walks on your left, if you're left handed your dog walks on your right. In an ideal world you should train your dog to walk on either side on command. 'Heel' for my dogs is on my left; 'Side' on my right; 'Tuck in' is walk behind me.

Why? Well it goes back to when the dogs were used as war dogs, armoured up and on the battle field. The soldiers would have their sword in their right hand (or left) and their dog on the opposite side. Nowadays when we shoot a right-handed 'gun' will have their dog on the left and vice versa.

I'm right handed so all the methods are detailed as I would do them with a dog on my left side; if your dog walks on your right simply reverse things.

Walking on a loose lead

For me walking on a loose lead is something that is expected of every dog; allowing your dog to pull is unfair on both you and your dog, you'll end up with shoulder, neck and back problems and so could your dog.

This is the routine that I use to teach people how to get their dogs to walk on a loose lead; it's an adaptation of the method I was shown by Noel Hutchinson when I lived in New Zealand. I find it's the quickest way to train a dog to walk nicely.

If you normally hold the lead in both your left and right hands then continue to do so for the time being; hold the lead with the handle loop over the thumb of your right hand and then close your hand around it. With your left hand hold the lead between 8 & 12 inches up from the collar (more if you have a small dog) so that there is a little slack in the lead between your hand and your dog's collar.

If you normally hold the lead in your right hand with your dog on your left, so that your lead drapes across the front of you, then continue to do so making sure that you have it long enough so that when you walk your legs aren't tightening the lead and checking your dog with each step that you take.

When all is calm, set off saying 'heel' in a cheery voice and when your dog is walking nicely beside you say 'good boy heel', again in a cheery voice.

If he moves ahead, drop the lead out of your left hand and step back giving the lead a quick double flick/a couple of fast gentle tugs with your right hand at the same time as turning 180 degrees to walk back the way you came giving your dog no choice other than to come with you. Take up the lead again with your left hand as detailed above and continue walking.... only when your dog is walking nicely do you talk to him.

To go back the way you came you can either repeat the exercise if your dog's ahead of you, or left turn and left turn again, walking across the front of your dog (rather than around him) which will encourage your dog behind the leg. If you do the left, left turn please make sure your legs are straight and you're taking little strides – so you're almost shuffling towards your dog, that way you'll be barging him out of the way rather than kneeing him (which we don't want). You're looking to do what another dog would which is barge him out of the way, also, because you're walking across the path of your dog, you're communicating that you're important enough to do so.

Repeat the above step as many times as it takes to get your dog walking with you on a loose lead – the first time may take a little while. Don't go for your walk until your dog is walking nicely... remember it's the behaviour that brings the reward and in this case going for a nice walk with you is the reward.

Always, always, always return to a loose lead. After every correction bring your dog back to a loose lead.

You can do the above holding the lead just in the left hand if you find it easier or when you get used to doing the routine and in preparation for when you train off lead walking. Put the handle over the thumb of your left hand and loop the lead up (almost so you're holding an 8 with your hand at its waist). Apply the same principles as detailed above using the left hand only.

Now before we go any further you need to be conversant with what I regard as a flick (or a gentle tug if that's easier to get your head around). Think about flicking water off a paintbrush after you've cleaned it; it's a fast downward flick, the emphasis being on fast rather than hard... that's the flick you use as a consequence for your dog.

By being fast rather than hard or pulling, you're mentally pulling your dog up short; you're not trying to hurt your dog or be mean to your dog, just pull him up short so that he knows in no uncertain terms that he has just received a consequence. Remember in the dog eat dog world of the canine, your dog knows he's doing the right thing when he hasn't been reprimanded by a senior rank.

Walking off lead

At some point you're going to want to be able to walk your dog off-lead and to heel without him taking off. It's a lot easier than it seems, the key funnily enough, is teaching your dog to always walk on a loose lead. If your dog is used to being by your leg without any pressure on his neck, he won't notice the difference when the lead is dropped; this is when you get to find out if you've been consistent with your dog walking to heel or not.

Find a secure place where you want to train off-lead walking. When your dog is pootling along nicely to heel, very quietly drop the lead and let your dog drag it behind him, talk to him as you go – you want his attention on you and not on some bunnies in the hedge. If your dog gets a little bit too far ahead pick up the lead, do a double flick and change direction; when he's walking nicely again drop the lead and then do a left about turn (or left turn, left turn) and continue with your walk. If your dog starts to fall behind, pick up the lead and pull him into the correct position; try not to glare at him or look at him while you're doing this as it may make him back off from you which is the opposite of what you're trying to achieve, when he's at heel, praise, continue walking and drop the lead.

In time you'll be able to just stand on the lead if your dog gets a bit ahead... step on and off without breaking your stride that way your dog will get a little correction without you having to bend down.

As with training any new exercise, little and often is the key; aim initially for 5-6 strides of your dog walking with the lead dragging, pick the lead up and after a couple of strides break off and play. Repeat the exercise regularly during your walk but only when it's safe to do so.

Another great way to train your dog to walk off-lead and to heel is to put your dog in a sit stay, do a small circle around him and as you pass him pat your leg and say "heel". Walk off with your dog to heel talking, praising and smiling; after a few paces pick up the lead then break off and play.

Playtime!

There's just something about watching a dog running free and doing his own thing that is incredibly appealing to humans. We just don't seem to be able to get enough of watching our dog prancing about and playing the fool; maybe it allows us to get in touch with our inner-child or maybe just the fact that we're relaxing and smiling watching our dog play releases happy hormones and lets the stress melt away.

Once you have your dog walking nicely to heel on and off lead, you'll no doubt want to think about giving your dog some play time... or not. What about if it goes wrong? We won't find it relaxing then, it can be one of the most stressful aspects of owning a dog. There are a number of things that you need to bear in mind when giving your dog 'playtime', however, unless you have trained your recall, if I was you, I wouldn't even be contemplating it.

Picture this: your gorgeous puppy followed you everywhere from when you first started to walk out, once you were on a field you'd let him off and he'd stay really close. Then as he got older, round about the five month mark, he'd start running out in front and pausing looking at you "yes, off you go" you'd say smiling distractedly as you were walking along talking to your friend. Sure enough 'off your dog went' and then a couple of months later you realised that when you let your dog off lead he went off and did his own thing, coming back on his own, sometimes without you even having to call him but more often than not, if there were other dogs around or those irresistible little furry things, you'd have to wait until your dog had had enough.

If you have a spaniel no doubt you wouldn't see him for dust and he would have grown cloth ears... Labradors are no better. Come to think of it no breed is, some will run back and forwards nose on the ground, some will take off and track, others will start mousing, others will scent mark, others will... you get the idea don't you? Once your dog has been encouraged to chase, track or scent there'll be no stopping him; every walk will be an out of control hunt.

So how did we go from beautifully behaved puppy to waiting for our dog to return at his leisure? Quite simple really, lack of leadership. When your young dog stopped and looked back at you he was doing one of a number of things; making sure he was on the right 'hunting' trail, trying to communicate to you that you were following an inferior track to his, making sure you were still following his lead, waiting for his pack to catch up, reassuring himself that he wasn't alone... you can see where this is going can't you. For you to then give your dog permission to continue was in effect saying that he was the better hunter and tracker (which he obviously is) and that he didn't need to be part of your hunting group. If at that time you'd taken control of the situation and called your dog to you, made him walk to heel or played with him then chances are you wouldn't have lost your recall. A trifling thing perhaps, but not for the dog who views life very differently.

Playtime involving other dogs can go wrong in other ways, not only could it lead to your dog learning to ignore you because he was having such a good time with the other dog, he could learn, through being mobbed into continuing to play by an unruly dog that you're not strong enough to deal with the situation and not as important as other dogs, it could also lead to your dog being fearful or aggressive.

A couple of years ago I used to walk with a friend and her dog. When her dog was in his formative months he had been to classes that allowed dogs to play and jump all over each other. As a result, her dog had learned no self control or canine etiquette. After a couple of times of her dog persisting to maul at my gentle goldie whilst he was lying on his back with his legs in the air, tail tucked in I stopped walking with her. Her dog could quite easily have taught my dog that the universal canine signal for "I give in/no more/don't hurt me/I'm not worthy" didn't work during play and my dog could, and I believe would, have used his weapons to get out of a situation he was very uncomfortable with. If I hadn't have stepped in to call an end to the play session then my dog would have had to take control of the situation and out of fear may have approached play sessions with other dogs in the same manner.

Playtime is great for you and playtime is great for your dog, but only if approached in the same manner as everything else you do with your dog and that is with you monitoring the play and taking control as necessary. The best playtime is balanced between your dog having some time to be in his nose and be a dog and playing with you and once you've got your retrieves trained you'll find playtime will take on a whole new meaning for you and your dog and your relationship will change out of all recognition.

Socialisation

As a behaviourist I see a lot of dogs that have been to 'socialisation' classes that allow the dogs to go charging up to each other, on lead and off, and play and bounce and run together with very little regard for the person at the end of the lead.

When those dogs (not all I hasten to add, but a lot) go out into the 'real' world they expect to be able to behave the same way and start lunging towards other dogs they meet in order to say hello and play. At first they may pull on the lead towards the other dog while the person at the end of the lead says something like "now it's not time to play, you're supposed to be walking with me, come on..." but really all they're saying is "yadda, yadda, yadda, blah, blah, blah" or to translate into canine "yes that's what I want you to do, you pull on the lead towards the other dog". Remember that to a dog, unless he's told otherwise his behaviour is deemed to be acceptable.

If you're lucky that's all that happens, a couple of strides and your dog is walking nicely to heel again. However, what generally happens is that next time you see a dog you tense up, the dog feels the tension, looks to see where the problem is, see's a dog and remembers being 'praised' for reacting last time and lunges rather than pulls...., again with the 'blah blah blah'. Next time you see a dog you tense up, the dog feels the tension and remembers being 'praised' for reacting last time and lunges up on his hind legs barking.... again with the 'blah blah blah'. Next time you see a dog... well you get the picture.

The next few pages are all about teaching your dog to behave in public so that you'll have a well mannered dog that you can be proud of taking anywhere.

Teaching your dog to do nothing

One of the first things I do when training someone is to show them how to teach their dog to do 'nothing'. Stand in a field with your dog hanging out beside you on a loose lead. If the dog starts to wander or mooch a quick double flick on the lead along with their name (in your normal voice, not a growl) will bring them back to you and praise when they're by your side. (This is where a name with 2 syllables is great - you flick on each syllable... Ro-flick ver-flick).

When you get your dog relaxing beside you wander off to a new place to repeat the exercise. Your dog learns really quickly that when you stop it's his job to chill out and relax beside you.

What does this have to do with socialisation? Well when you meet someone in the street you stand still and do nothing. Your dog will have learned the 'drill' and will relax. Your dog learns to take his cue from you and when you relax he follows suit; whether that's on the street, in the pub or on the shooting field.

Meeting and Greeting
Passing on a street
Because we're primates we tend to do everything 'straight on'. We go straight in facing the person, eyeball to eyeball, hand outstretched ready to shake or hug and pat pat on the back. When we sit with a friend it's opposite sides of the table, again eyeball to eyeball chest facing chest.

For a dog however, not only is this breaking the canine etiquette rules it's intimidating and out-and-out rude. Dogs prefer to 'curve gently' into meeting another dog, turning the head to one side and catching eye contact for part of a second. As they approach they'll drop their eyes, bow their head and slightly turn away. As they come together they're generally head to tail, shoulder to shoulder with a gap between them as they sniff each other. They'll then either curve around each other a bit more, have a good sniff, invite one another to play, hump, dominate or walk on by.

So how do we pass another dog on a street? Well, you introduce the gentle curve by working out your line of approach as soon as you see the other dog. The easiest way to do this is to make sure you pass handler to handler rather than dog to dog. So it goes dog handler handler dog; that way there is a gap between the dogs and as you approach you curve around those coming in the opposite direction. To start with keep walking, don't stop to chat.... you've honoured both dogs and not forced a confrontation by making them approach eyeball to eyeball and chances are they found out everything they needed to know about each other at 50 paces.

Stopping for a chat
Once you've gotten your dog chilling out and doing nothing and walking past dogs on the street then stop for a natter.

Approach the dog as above and if you know the person well (what I'd recommend is you talked over the phone to your dog pals and arranged a walk past, then a chat, then a walk together) pop your dog into a sit and shake their hand. If your dog gets up gently, but with authority, put him back into a sit. When they're sitting nicely do a one armed hug, again reaffirming the 'sit' from your dog. After your natter continue with your walk; if your dog has sat quietly 'doing nothing' on a loose lead then by all means let them sniff each other, but only if you know the other dog is okay too. Don't ever feel obliged to let your dog say 'hello' either because you feel guilty to your dog for not letting him or because the other person wants their dog to say hello. I've been accused of having unhappy dogs because I wouldn't let them run riot with an out of control chocolate lab.... yeah right!

If either of the dogs start putting their heads across the other dog's back, shoulder or neck it's time to get them back by your leg in a sit; likewise if their tail starts to go erect and they tuck their head up with chin in or they flatten their ears back against their head. These are all signs that your dog's getting amorous or may try to mount the other dog. Learn to read your dog and you'll have happier walks.

Going for a walk with a mate

If you and your friend have both got happy go lucky dogs then once you've said hello you can just go for a walk side by side (dog handler dog handler or dog handler handler dog). Providing your dogs are walking nicely to heel on a loose lead you can, for the most part, ignore them and enjoy your walk, however, if your dog starts getting ahead, you owe it to your dog to correct him there and then and turn the walk into a socialisation walking session (to me socialisation is about teaching a dog to relax in the company of other dogs not to let them behave like loonies with each other).

If you've got a dog that's not a 100% with others or if it's a new dog and you're 'checking them out' then do some parallel walking first.

Arrange to meet on neutral territory or if you're walking on a common try to walk parallel with someone in the distance, so that you're walking in the same direction as them with a big gap between you (side on rather than them in front). As you walk reduce the distance between you... don't try and get closer than a street width to start off with if the other dog is a stranger or if either of you are having problems with your dog's behaviour. When you can parallel walk comfortably a street widths apart reduce the gap until it's a pavement distance and then side by side.

Bringing a strange dog into your home

If you know the dog, and the dogs know each other but he's never been to your home, then bring him in on lead and keep him on lead for a few minutes before letting him off, however, if either of the dogs are unknown characters then the best thing you can do is parallel walk them until you are walking side by side.

Go into the house in the order of the owner of the house followed by their dog, followed by the 'new' handler and dog; go straight into the garden. Chill out with the dogs doing nothing, then, in the same order go in to the house. Hang around in a room relaxing and doing nothing with both dogs by your side still on lead. When they're relaxed drop the lead and 'chill'. Remember to honour the dog's body language and avoid having them lying eyeball to eyeball. If they get up to greet each other stay relaxed, maybe with a foot near their dangling

lead just in case - this is where you have to read the situation for yourself.
If you get up to leave the room take your dog with you on lead. When they're totally relaxed with each other remove the leads... or not, there is no rush leave it until next time.

If the dogs are completely at ease with each other let them have a play by all means but remember that you are the one in control of the situation and if it looks like one dog can't be bothered or is getting a bit exuberant tell them to calm down and have them by you again.

Remember other people's spoiled dogs are just as much a pain as other people's spoiled children. When you walk your dog, you and he are part of the primate/canine society and it is up to you to teach him to be a well mannered member that can be taken anywhere - I find that if you're consistent with the above, not only will your dog become much more relaxed you'll have just that... a dog you can take anywhere and be welcomed back.

Recall

This is such a sticking point. It shouldn't be but it is.

As far as I'm concerned either your dog comes when called (or whistled) and has a recall or it doesn't come when called, in which case it hasn't. The amount of times I've asked people how their dog's recall is and they say "good". After a bit of probing I find out that the recall is good if they're in the middle of no-where, there are no distractions and they have a bag of chicken... hmmm no recall then?

Your dog should recall 99% of the time, the other 1% should be when you inadvertently called him while he's toileting! To let your dog off lead when you don't have a reliable recall is not only irresponsible, it is dangerous.

You should know where your dog is and what he's doing at all times and be ready to step in when you see fit. I always try very hard not to anthropomorphise the dog, however, sometimes in order to understand the mentality of the animal that you're dealing with you have to...so, imagine your dog is a child under the age of four that can't communicate properly and hasn't yet reached the stage in their life when they can be reasoned with (I know parents of teenagers will be thinking, like I am writing this, "you mean they reach a point where you can reason with them?"). Would you let that child run off for hours on end, out of sight, playing with other children that you didn't know... of course you wouldn't. Yet time and time again I hear of people letting their dogs off in the woods and take the same route back to the car to so that the dog can find them or meet up with them at the car.

I live not far from Salisbury plain where people turn up with their dog, open the boot and read a book or take a stroll whilst waiting for the dog to have their fun and return to them up to two or three hours later. These dogs are known as 'plains' dogs to the trainers in the area. It's not just on the plains that this is happening; the local forest is full of similar cases.

You may be thinking, how shocking, how awful etc., or you may be thinking, hmmm I do that, however, it's not necessarily the owners faults. Over the last decade we've been brainwashed by trainers who think that dogs don't need rules, let alone rules enforced, and that we must always train positively and with bits of chicken. I agree with the positive training and high value rewards but, dogs do need rules and they need them enforcing. To have a dog any other way is to either turn him into a plains dog or a dog that's never let off the lead for fear of him not coming back.

You've already made the commitment to changing the way your dog behaves otherwise you wouldn't still be reading, so commit your dog to having a great recall and for the foreseeable future train your dog to the whistle and use a long line. Some dogs have a good recall after a month, some after two and sometimes you have to periodically return to the line.

Working with a line

A long line is just that; it can be a bought line from a pet shop which generally come in lengths of 10m and 15m, a lunge line that you use with horses or it can be a homemade one of rope and spring clip attached. I made my first long line from bale twine when I was 13, it must have been at least 300 yards long as it stretched quite easily from one side of the hayfield to the other – I just tied it on to my dog's collar with a well practiced slipknot and removed it when I put her lead back on. Whatever you use just remember not to tie yourself up on it and never let it lie on the ground behind your legs and, if like my first one it's made of thin twine, wear gloves.

Walk on a loose lead to a suitable field or area where you want to give your dog some freedom. Attach the long-line (then remove the lead) and walk for about 50 yards or so with your dog by your side on a loose lead. Give your release command and let your dog out up to the length of the long-line.

The line must never have tension... as your dog gets towards the end of the long-line, give it a quick flick and say "Dog come" or "Dog this way". If you say the "come" command then bring your dog to you and give a food reward. If it's "this way", allow him to walk with you at a distance and give verbal praise.

If your dog's too far ahead of you give the line a quick flick and say "Dog too far". Verbally praise as he comes back within a decent range.

Do the above on every walk for 2 weeks. On the 3rd week drop the line and allow your dog to drag it behind him... not only will it slow him down a bit but if he doesn't respond immediately you can stand on the long-line for immediate control.

If you feel confident with the recall at week 4, then remove the long-line otherwise continue letting your dog drag the line behind him until you're confident.

Never do long-line training in the forest or where there are a lot of bushes as it would be really easy for your dog to get caught up and hurt his neck and back. Use the long-line training plan in conjunction with training your dog to the whistle so that by the time you take the long-line off you should have a dog that returns as soon as he hears peep-peep.

Don't be shy with your praise - the more exuberant the better. Don't be afraid to use a jackpot (many treats one after the other each accompanied with a "good dog") when training a recall and always use high value treats. When you give your dog a food reward, give the treat with one hand and stroke him with the other. Remember he's not allowed to run off again without permission.

You always want your dog to come and be stroked when you call him to you as you want to get your dog into the habit of coming right up and not dancing around slightly out of reach.

The Whistle recall

Here follows a little training programme to condition your dog to a whistle. What you're doing is putting a little picture in your dog's brain associating the sound of the whistle with lots of food (it's based on Pavlovian (as in Pavlov's dog), or classical conditioning). As each week goes by we add more pictures and change them slightly so that your dog associates the whistle with being by your side.

For 2 weeks peep-peep on the whistle immediately before you put your dog's dinner down for him to eat. If you normally make your dog wait for a couple of seconds before releasing him to eat his meal, then, as you release him to eat, peep-peep on the whistle.

Week 3, as well as above start taking your whistle on your walk and after you've called your dog in the normal manner (that is without the whistle) and he's by your side, peep-peep and give a treat.

Week 4, continue using the whistle at mealtimes and now peep-peep plus name for recall when out and about. Treat when by side.

Week 5, peep-peep for recall and phase out treats. Remember to give occasionally though as if there's a one in 5 chance of a treat, the dog, with his "what's in it for me attitude" will come back eagerly.

Any whistle will do providing it's not a silent one – you want to know that your dog has heard it so you can decide if he's 'dicking about' or not.

When training recalls, remember to always use a high value reward either cheese or chopped up cocktail sausages or something equally tasty; make it fun; make yourself interesting; add a consequence for not coming (flick on the long-line) and a consequence for coming (stroke, scratch, sweetie).

Sit

When teaching your dog to sit, it's important to teach him not only to sit in front of you but also on either side of you as well as on lots of different surfaces.

Dogs don't learn the same way that we do – for them the command is associated not only with action and textures but also the picture they get in their brain as they're learning the command.

I've taught lots of owners where they'll be quite happily walking their dogs beautifully to heel but as soon as they stop and tell their dog to sit the dog scoots around and sits very nicely about a foot in front of them gazing up intently waiting for their food reward.

While this shows the dog has been trained, it also shows that the dog hasn't been trained in the real world and only at home or in a village hall. You need to be able to stop, put your dog in a sit and then move off again without clattering all over your dog and falling flat on your face in the process.

Remember when training a new exercise to keep the sessions short and end on a high. Two good sits are worth a lot more than ten mediocre ones: quality not quantity is what you aim for when training your dog. After each training session either play with your dog or give them a good stroke/scratch/massage... and smile; your dog will remember the 'warm and fuzzy' at the end of the training session and will be keen for the next one.

Training the sit: with food

Training the sit initially is done with food and with your dog facing you.

Take a treat between your index finger and thumb with the rest of your fingers straight but not splayed. Hold the sweetie just above your dog's head and, in an up and over movement, slowly take the food towards the dog's hind quarters. As your dog puts his backside down quietly say "sit", then praise and treat.

Don't move the food too fast or your dog will jump up. If you go straight back with the treat rather than in an 'up and over' movement, your dog will walk backwards or spin around to try and get the treat. Remember, if you're using food, your dog only gets the treat when he's done the behaviour you're trying to train, in this instance when his backside and his two front paws are on the ground.

If your dog starts to go into the sitting position as you start to lift the food then you can change it from training the 'sit' to commanding the 'sit'. Hold the treat as above and as you start to raise your hand say 'sit', as your dog's backside hits the ground say 'sit' again and then reward.

Once your dog is sitting nicely draw out how long it is between you saying 'sit' and your dog getting the reward. Now is the time to start withholding the treat and to start phasing them out to one in five using your voice and gentle, calm stroking as a reward for compliance instead.

Why quietly? Well if you train your dog using a sergeant major voice you'll always have to use a sergeant major voice. Much better to train commands using a calm, quiet voice then, if you ever have to use your lungs to get your dog's attention, then oh boy will you get his attention.

What's with holding the treat in a certain way? By holding the treat in a 'pincer' grip and the rest of your fingers straight, you're preparing your gundog for the sit/stop hand signal. When you stop training with food all you'll need to do is straighten out your index finger and you have a conditioned hand signal, similar to the one used by a policeman to stop traffic.

Once your dog is happily obeying the 'sit' command and will sit in front of you it's time to teach him to sit by your side. With your dog on lead, manoeuvre yourself so that your dog is to your left heel. Using your lead (in your left hand) if necessary to stop your dog moving forward, hold a treat in your right hand as described above and twist so that you can do the same up and over movement with your hand as your dog is by your side.

Once your dog is happily sitting on command to your left manoeuvre yourself so that your dog is to your right heel. Using your lead (in your right hand) if necessary to stop your dog moving forward, hold a treat in your left hand as described above and twist so that you can do the same up and over movement with your hand as your dog is by your side.

Training the sit: without food

This is the routine you go through once your dog knows what "sit" means and chooses to ignore you. I would imagine that this would happen, more often than not whilst you're out walking with your dog, you stop and tell your dog to sit and your dog is distracted. Rather than tell your dog to sit again put your dog in a sit.

Using your right hand gently lift up the lead lifting your dog's head up with it, with your left hand ease his back end down by putting gentle pressure to the left of the spine at the point where the ribs have just finished – by gently squeezing the area at the last rib and pushing down towards his bum your dog will sit (this feels a bit like someone rubbing our bottom rib, try it, you'll collapse into the pressure which is what we want your dog to do). As your dog starts to put his backside down say "sit", release the pressure and praise. (If you're training your dog to sit on your right hand side then you'd use the right hand side of the spine instead, the side that is furthest away from your leg). Also, when you lift up the lead it should only be enough to lift your dog's head up, no more as you could damage his neck.

Never put pressure on the sacrum or hips area because if your dog resists the pressure and you continue to push you could hurt him.

Remember you should only ask your dog to do something once, whether that's sit, down, come etc., bear in mind that if your dog is used to you saying "sit" 10 times before you make him do it then not only will the command become "sit sit sit sit sit sit sit SIT SIT SIT", but your dog will learn he can ignore the first nine words that come out of your mouth which will play havoc with your recall.

*Gently lift up the lead whilst at the same time ease his back end down
by putting gentle pressure to the side of the spine where the ribs have just finished*

By gently squeezing the area at the last rib and pushing down towards his bum your dog will sit

Training the whistle sit

Once your dog understands and is following the sit command every time you give it, it's time to train the whistle sit.

Every time you stop, tell your dog to sit and make sure he sits first time. Once he's in a sit do a single 'pip' on your whistle as you take your right hand round to give the sit hand signal.

After a couple of weeks when you stop, pip on the whistle; your dog should sit. If you've been consistent, in another couple of weeks your dog will automatically sit when you stop.

Training your dog to stop on the whistle

Once your dog is sitting nicely to the whistle when you stop you need to expand the complexity in preparation for a whistle stop.

Use the whistle sit as you prepare to stop, instead 'half stop', give a hand signal for sit and keep moving. If the dog gets up lead him back to where you peeped. If your dog stays go back to your dog and make a big fuss, have a play and repeat.

Build up so that you're only faltering in your step as you give the sit whistle. Remember every time your dog gets it right to reward with a sweetie, a cuddle, a stroke or a play.

When your dog's ambling around the house, say "sit", give the hand signal and walk intently towards your dog. Once your dog sits, give a single peep on the whistle then drop the hand signal, change your energy from hard to soft, walk up to your dog and give him a stroke with lots of praise.

When your dog sits at distance as above use the whistle instead; if your dog doesn't respond immediately growl "sit" and walk at your dog until he does and then release the pressure immediately as above and reward.

Once your dog is happily doing all of the above it's time to do it outdoors... my advice would be to start in the garden before you do it in the park. Let your dog mooch around the garden. Have your whistle in your mouth and make yourself a bit interesting so your dog wants to wander over without any real urgency. As your dog approaches, peep on the whistle as you give the sit/stop hand signal and walk intently to your dog giving off the energy that to disobey wouldn't end well for the dog. As soon as your dog complies, drop the pressure, smile and tell him what a very good dog he is. If he doesn't comply then just continue to walk at him growling "sit" until he does... you've got it, the second he does the pressure is off.

When your dog is comfortable stopping on an ad-hoc basis, set him up to do a recall and as he approaches step forward into the stop routine as detailed above. When doing a formal recall with a stop it's important not to over-train the exercise as it can cause your dog to be a bit sticky on the recall which is the last thing you want. Instead do eight or nine normal recalls and slip in an occasional "stop".

Down

In the gundog world the down command is generally not taught. You want your gundog to see the action and be ready to move instantly you give a command which is the reason why, more often than not, it's omitted from the gundog's education.

However, first and foremost we're training the family pet which happens to be a gundog breed and so, the down, which is one of the most valuable things you can teach your dog, is detailed below. In an emergency it is sometimes easier to get your dog to respond to 'down' than it is to 'come', especially when he's in mid chase – your dog doesn't have to take his eyes off whatever he's chasing just lie down, whereas to come back to you means changing direction and 'giving up' the hunt.

Training the down: with food

Training the down, like the sit, is initially done with food and with your dog facing you. To make it easy for you and to save your back, sit on the floor with your dog. Put a couple of treats in your hand with your hand closed into a fist (knuckles up). Place your hand between/in front of your dog's front legs. As he bows fold him into a down with the other hand by gently pushing on his raised backend – push away from you rather than straight down; put the heel of your hand on or just behind his shoulders increase the pressure from shoulders towards his pelvis and you'll find he should drop into the position.

When he's in the down position release a treat as you remove your hand and say "down" followed by "good boy, down". If he stays down for a couple of seconds give him a second treat and again say "down" followed by "good boy, down". Release him from the exercise with a rapid stroke.

Remember, if you're using food, your dog only gets the treat when he's done the behaviour your trying to train, in this instance when he's in the down position.

When your dog starts to down when you move your hand towards the floor you can start changing your position as you teach it so instead of sitting on the floor, crouch, then bend down and then do it from standing upright. During this transition from floor to standing up your dog will start pre-empting your command and you can change it from training the down to commanding the down.

Once your dog is downing nicely draw out how long it is between you saying down and your dog getting the reward. Now is the time to start withholding the treat and starting to phase them out to one in five using your voice and gentle, calm stroking as a reward for compliance instead.

Place your hand between/ in front of your dog's front legs.
As he bows fold him into a down with the other hand

Push away from you rather than straight down and you'll find he should 'drop' into the position

Put the treat on the ground and let him eat it

Training a 'snappy' down

I've found that the best way of training a snappy down is by using a toy. Once your dog has the gist of what a down is, take his favourite toy and tell him to down. The second he's in the down position throw the toy for him making silly 'play' noises as you do and encourage your dog to play with his toy. Whenever my dogs have earned a toy I go 'yeeha' which is a cue for them to run around like loony's shaking the toy and prancing about with it.

As your dog realises that he gets his toy and lots of fun as soon as he's in the down position he'll start throwing himself on the ground ready for his reward. It's now that you can up the ante and only give him the toy if you think the down was fast enough – if it wasn't get him up and do it again. The key to this exercise is to keep it fun and exciting; train it indoors and then take a small toy out with you on walks and practice it in the real world.

Stay v Wait

I'm asked over and over again when to use the word 'stay' and when to use the word 'wait' as part of training a gundog. Well, up until a few years ago there was no such thing as either in the gundog world; when a gundog trainer said 'sit' they meant "sit until I tell you to move". All very well if you have a dog that lives outside or inside with just you. Once you start introducing other people into the equation it becomes quite impractical.

Just imagine you've spent weeks if not months training your dog to sit on command and remain in a sit until you say otherwise. Your great Aunt Mabel comes to stay for a week and keeps telling your dog to sit before she gives him a stroke and then wanders off to make a cup of tea, watch the telly or have an afternoon nap. Eventually your dog gets up and moves around and hey, guess what? No consequence for doing so. Remember how the dog thinks, if nothing bad happens he must be doing the right thing. Congratulations Aunt Mabel, you've just successfully broken months of training and taught the dog that sit doesn't mean sit/stay.

No, much better to let everyone use the sit command and you keep the more powerful 'stay' and 'wait' commands for yourself.

So what are the differences; well for me 'wait' means wait there, there's another command coming; whereas 'stay' means stay there until I come back to you.

I never ask a dog to get up and come to me after I've given a stay command and only ever release them after I've been back by their side for a few seconds: to release your dog immediately could make him anticipate the reward and get up to meet you on the way back.

'Wait', I would use if I was setting a dog up to train a recall or if I wanted my dog to wait while I set up some dummies for him to retrieve and I wasn't going to return to his side.

Training the stay

Once your dog is sitting nicely on command it's time to introduce them to the concept of staying. I do tend to train the stay in a different way to training the wait, although essentially they are in effect the same thing; that is, the dog doesn't move until you say otherwise. As noted above, with the stay you're returning to the dog whereas with the wait the dog is going to be moving without awaiting your return.

Start with your dog on his lead and sitting to heel. Use the 'sit' hand signal and say "stay", very quietly take a step to the side away from your dog and repeat the 'stay' command with signal. Count to three and return to your dog's side. On return repeat the 'stay' command, count to three and then release your dog with a play or a food reward or both. This may seem like going back to the beginning or being overly simple but, although your dog knows the 'sit' command by this point, he doesn't know 'stay' and you have to let him build up to that.

It's important not to try and rush your dog with the 'stay' command, hence stepping to the side rather than walking out in front. By stepping sideways your dog won't feel he's being left behind or abandoned and he'll learn that it's okay to sit away from your leg.

When your dog is happy and confident, step two paces to the side, again for three seconds and then repeat the return routine. When your dog is happy and confident, step in front of your dog, repeat the stay command and step back to the end of your lead repeating the stay command and counting to five before you return.

You continue in this manner until you can drop the lead and walk a few paces either to the side or to the front for 30 seconds. Congratulations you've trained a stay, now you need to refine it and then do some distraction training.

Refining the stay

You can refine and stretch the stay in many different ways and I've listed my favourites and the reasons why they are. Providing you take it steadily and keep the pressure off your dog as you make the 'stay' more challenging you'll end up with a really steady pet gundog.

Remember at the beginning of each exercise give a clear stay command and hand signal, at the end of each exercise make your dog wait for a couple of seconds before releasing him.

There and back again. Is as you may have guessed walking away and leaving your dog, getting to a set point in your mind (could be 5 paces or 50), doing an about turn and returning to your dog's side. One of the problems that I encountered when I trained my Labrador was creeping or standing up and readjusting himself and then sitting back down before I turned around and looked at him... not the biggest problem in the world, however I was doing obedience trials and competitions at the time and he would lose all his marks. The way that I got round it was by using a little handbag mirror or any little mirror you can slip in your pocket. As you walk away from your dog use it as you would a car mirror to see over your shoulder and check what your dog is doing; the second he moves go back to him and put him on the spot you left him on. He'll soon realise that he can't get away with anything, even a little bum shuffle, and will stop doing it – remember he's an animal and all animals, regardless of species, will only continue a behaviour if it benefits them. Rather than using a mirror you can set your dog up so he's facing a glass door and you can see his reflection as you leave him – training in the garden facing French windows works a treat.

Halfs and quarters. Walk away from your dog in a straight line, turn left after 5-10 paces and start walking a circle; as you get parallel to your dog return to your dog's side. Repeat to the right. This little exercise will get your dog used to you moving around during the stay and returning on a different path.

The circle. Start as if you're going to do a quarter or a half circle but instead continue all the way around stopping when you get in front of your dog again. This is to teach your dog confidence when you go out of sight. You need to decide if it's acceptable that, when you're out of sight your dog gets up and turns around to see you rather than just looking over his shoulder. If it's acceptable fine, if not you need to gently escort your dog so he's facing the original direction and repeat the exercise, maybe making your circle smaller and reassuring your dog with an extra 'stay' command as you move out of his field of vision. For me, I would always correct as stay means stay, regardless of where I am.

Being silly. There can be no greater way of training your dog to be steady in a stay than being silly; apart from that it's really good fun and if you're training with a mate you get to have a laugh at and with each other. Only your imagination will hold you back. Things that I do to train steadiness, with my dogs and with the groups that train with me are... jumping jacks, jogging around the dog, touching toes, sitting on the ground and clapping my hands and knees; in groups you can be a lot more inventive and we jog between and in front of the dogs, do a bit of highland jigging, playing pat-a-cake with each other and stand around gossiping and laughing.

The feint. When you return to your dog don't stop beside him, instead repeat the stay command as you get level and walk straight past him stopping about 5 paces behind. Return to your dog's side, or not it's really up to you, you can go stand in front of him again and repeat the exercise without releasing him in between. This will teach your dog to wait to be released rather than presuming he's going to be able to get up when you return to him.

Stretching the stay. In terms of both distance and duration. Walk away for five or so paces and turn to face your dog. If your dog can happily do a thirty second sit stay then after twenty seconds repeat the stay command and take two steps back. After ten seconds repeat the stay command and take two steps back. After another ten seconds repeat the stay command and take two steps back. After another ten seconds repeat the stay command and move forwards towards your dog to the original starting stay position, after another ten seconds return to your dog; this means your dog will, in total, have done a one minute sit stay.

This will very quickly not only increase the time and duration of your stays but will also help your dog to focus on you and not let his mind wander as he'll never quite know what you're going to do next. You can do it in increments of five seconds, twenty second or five paces it really is about evaluating what your dog is comfortable with at this moment in time and slightly stretching it. If your dog gets up then you know you've overdone it too quickly, set your dog up and do a 'baby' stay so that your dog gets to end the session with praise.

Training the wait

You can train the wait in a less business-like manner than the stay. Pop your dog in a sit, and with the 'sit' hand signal very clearly say "wait". Step in front of your dog and say "wait" again and step back until you're at the end of his lead. Count to three (or four or ten) and with a big smile call your dog to you and give him lots of praise for coming. If your dog tries to stand up and move towards you before you've called him, just tell him "no" and put him back on the spot and repeat the exercise. I tend to reinforce the wait when playing and training the retrieve rather than getting overly serious which I do with the stay command as for me the stay could save my dog's life. Another reason for not getting too serious and growly with the wait is that you want your dog to be keen the second you tell him to move, whether that's for a recall or a retrieve and if you get too serious training the wait you could end up with a 'sticky' dog that's unsure coming when called and that's the last thing we want!

Not You

Another command that I use a lot that you may find valuable with your dog is 'not you'. It means quite simply that you don't want your dog to come with you but it doesn't have to hold a position. It's great if you tie your dog up, you just walk away and say 'not you' – your dog is then free to sit, stand, lie or move around without getting into trouble for breaking a command.

Rather than say 'stay' when you leave a room and don't want your dog to follow you (which will break the effectiveness of your 'stay' command) say 'not you', put your hand in front of your dog's face so that you're blocking him from moving forward and then move off without him.

Likewise when you leave a room and are planning on closing the door behind don't say anything, just leave otherwise you are 'wasting' a command.

It's easier to train the 'not you' exercise at a door way or when going from one texture to another as the dog will appreciate the doorway commands respect and will recognise the change in texture under his paws.

Walk into a room with your dog beside you, as you cross the threshold reach down with your open hand in front of your dog's face, say "not you" and push towards your dog; your dog may continue walking in which case gently push their face backwards, say "not you!" and keep walking. Your dog will stop at the threshold. If he crosses it then 'herd' him out of the room and again say "not you!" Your dog will very quickly get the message that when you say "not you!" he's not allowed to follow you into the room. This is very different to 'stay' as the dog is allowed to do whatever he wants providing he doesn't follow you into the room.

Leave it!

This exercise has deliberately been left to the end of the training section to emphasise that in a training session this is always done last and preferably in isolation to any other training that you're doing. Because when you first train a new exercise, to make it easier for the dog to understand what is required, you use a bit of food; the last thing you want is to do is to teach him to turn his nose in the air when food is on offer and then expect to be able to use it to lure and train... do yourself, and your dog, a favour and train nothing new for an hour or so after 'playing' leave it.

For this exercise you'll need some very high value treats, cocktail sausages, cheese or something that's equally tasty. Hold the treat in a pinch grip between your thumb and middle finger. Offer your dog a treat and gently say "Good, take it". Do this at least five times.

Then offer your dog a treat and do not say anything. When he goes to take the treat, gently tap his nose with your index finger and gently say "leave it". Your dog will either try again to take the treat, in which case you'll tap his nose and say "leave it" again or he'll ever so slightly pull back or turn his face to the side. At that point you'll drop your index finger and say "Good, take it". The second your dog decides that the treat isn't worth the hassle he gets it.

Do this exercise as many times as you can throughout the day until all you have to do is lift your index finger up as he goes to take the sweetie and he backs off. You can then make it more challenging by moving the sweetie towards him repeating the exercise; it won't take long before he physically moves his body away from the sweetie, when he does make a really big fuss of him as well as giving him the food.

This is the action that you're training, you raise your index finger and say 'leave it' in a normal tone of voice and your dog moves away from whatever he is doing. How valuable is this going to be; no more having to worry about the dog stealing things from children's hands, picking something up off a table or eating the irresistible sheep pooh!

Try not to use this if your dog has something in his mouth until after you've trained a really good retrieve though; if he's carrying something you always want his first thought to be "got something in my mouth, who can I give it to", instead call him to you and take it off him with praise.

Where and when to train your Dog
"Where and when don't you?"

Every time you interact with your dog you're training him on one level or another. Let's just say for example, you're settling down for the night to watch a movie and you tell your dog to go on his bed. He meanders over to it and lies just in front of it but not actually on it, what do you do?

Well you can ignore it which means that you've successfully communicated to your dog that when you're relaxing on the settee your dog can more or less do what he wants, or you can repeat the command, in which case you're telling your dog the first command doesn't count, or, you can get up and either 'herd' your dog onto his bed or you can 'escort' your dog on to his bed using his collar. Many different responses each one training your dog – for me there is no response other than to herd or escort them to their bed. When I tell my dogs to do something it's not negotiable, whether that's in the field or the front room. ('Escorting' your dog to his bed doesn't mean to drag him along by his collar, it's simply keeping a steady pressure that doesn't allow him the choice of going anywhere other than where you want him to be; remember dogs don't 'pull' other dogs around, they tend to push or apply pressure.)

You don't need a big field or access to a special area to train your dog, well not initially anyway. Basic training should be a part of life when you have a dog; try to incorporate as much training into your daily routine as possible. When you put the kettle on for example, put your dog in a sit-stay, when the adverts come on the telly put your dog in a sit-stay, I trained my Labrador his sit-stays when I did the ironing... starting off with a t-shirt I built it up to a quilt cover and then three or four items. By making it part of your routine you won't feel as if you're running out of time to train and your dog learns that when you say stay you mean it, regardless of what else you're doing.

I also trained both my dogs all the various elements of the retrieve, including more advanced stuff, in the front room armed with dummies, toys and a handful of treats. Be inventive and creative; when we cover the various gundog training exercises there'll be examples of how to incorporate it indoors as well as out and I always recommend you train indoors first without distraction before you venture out into the real world.

When training my dogs to walk off lead I would heel them to the garden, put them in a sit-stay while I hung out the washing and then heel them back in through the back door, releasing them with a play in the kitchen.

Training will progress much quicker if you do it in small chunks and only push the dog when you're both in a place mentally and physically to learn. Keep it fun, slightly challenging and have a plan for the training session. Maybe one session concentrate on training the sit another concentrate on training the down. Initially aim for each training session to last five minutes or so building up to about fifteen. Going for marathon training sessions will just tire you both out and it will turn into hard work rather than having fun.

Always try to end on a high, if things start to go wrong or your dog isn't 'getting' it, then rather

Bart saw something I didn't; when I sent him he "went for it!"

than keeping on and on at the same thing, change it ever so slightly to make it easier for your dog, give him heaps of praise and call it a day... remember your dog can get an A+ for effort.

Remember when you're with your dog you're doing one of three things

- Training him a new exercise in which case you keep your tone of voice gentle and take things slowly and reward him with praise, strokes and sweeties

- Giving a command in which case you calmly and quietly but with authority tell your dog to do something, reward with praise and a stroke

- Reinforcing an existing one in which case you take on a 'no nonsense' attitude of aloof silence and escort your dog back, 'no' in an authoritative voice to pre-empt the misdemeanour or growl AHHHHH to pull your dog up short for 'dicking about'. Remember though you must always check that your dog actually understands what's expected of him before applying discipline otherwise it's not fair on the dog and you'll feel bad about it later

I don't think that we can ever say "that's it I've trained my dog, all done!" I think that the most we can ever aim for is "I have a really well trained dog" (thinking silently "at the minute").

Because we're dealing with a living, breathing, thinking being that has an innate attitude of "what's in it for me?" we can never presume that training is over and we're just maintaining a 'steady state'; the opportunist that is your dog will look for an opening to do as he pleases and will take it, unless of course he knows, through experience, that there is a consequence involved and has developed self control.

Bringing out the best in your Pet Gundog

There are many different breeds of gundogs, from the instantly recognisable Labrador and Springer Spaniel to the recognisable but "are you sure that's a gundog?" Weimaraners and Irish Water Spaniels... and everything in between; including the 'newer editions' of the Springadors and Cockapoos.

All gundogs: all great pet dogs (although some will be more challenging than others): all dogs.

When I train gundogs I always try to address the animal first (the dog) and then the individual while bearing in mind the type or breed. For every dog, regardless of breed, I start by expecting good behaviour all round as described in previous chapters, training the basics of walking on a loose lead, sit, whistle recall and walking to heel off lead.

So that's the 'dog' element taken care of. Then it's the gundog element... the retrieve. Even if you have a spaniel that runs around in his nose all of the time the retrieve can be a godsend. Just imagine if you could do something that would take your dog out of his nose in a moment and have his attention back on you. Well that is the power of a well trained and thoughtfully trained retrieve.

Once you've trained your retrieve you can then have fun with the breed element for example having your spaniel 'hunt' for you on walks or your retriever going back the way you came to pick things up for you. Not only will you be fulfilling your dog's needs from a breed point of view but you'll also be tiring your dog out mentally and physically and in all honesty, a tired dog is a happy dog, a contented and well behaved dog.

Although the breeds are grouped by Retriever, Spaniels (Hunting Retriever), Pointers and Setters and HPRs, breeds and individuals vary within the group which is why it's important to build up a bond with your dog and see what works for them and what doesn't. For example Labrador Retrievers tend to scent with their noses very low skimming the grass while running whereas the Golden Retriever tends to air-scent until the last minute when they may, or may not, drop their heads. Likewise with individuals; some Labradors that train with me are bold, some are brave, some are nervy, some are bolshie; some spaniels are timid, some are physically fast, some are physically slow, some are fast learners, some are slow learners; the list really is endless.

The training techniques that follow are, as the title implies, for the pet gundog and so it is a basic 'one size fits all' approach to gundog training. The best way to use this section of the book is to read it all the way through and then start training; that way you'll know what's coming and what you're going to be aiming for.

Before we start you may be wondering what equipment you need to invest in, well you already have your dog which is a good start; a collar and lead, although slip leads do tend to be used, especially when you have your dogs working through bushes as you would take the collar off to prevent them getting caught up, in the early days whilst training the retrieve you'll need a collar to attach the long line to; a long line at a minimum length of 10 metres, a homemade made line if you feel inclined is perfect as it can be of any length; a whistle on a lanyard, my preference is a 211 and a ½ just because it's easier on my ears; a simple canvas dummy, I would recommend you start with a pencil puppy dummy and build up to a 1lb canvas dummy and tennis balls, tennis balls and more tennis balls as well as a play toy and some treats.

No doubt the names of the equipment sound double-dutch to you. I can remember placing my first gundog equipment order. The internet wasn't as popular as it is now and if you wanted to place an order with a company you had to look them up in the Yellow Pages and give them ring. So, I phoned up and very confidently said "I'd like a lanyard and an eleven and half acme gundog whistle please" (along with my dummies). When the gent on the other side of the phone repeated my order he gave it the full name of a 211 and a half. "No" was my reply "I only want one". I could hear his smothered sniggers as he composed himself enough to tell me that the proper name was two eleven and a half as it indicated the pitch and tone of the pitch than a 10 for example. Thank goodness I have a sense a humour... I laughed it off as one of my blonde moments.

The Puppy Retrieve

Now you have a well mannered and well trained dog at home it's time to turn our attention to the retrieve. There are many aspects of training your dog to work as a gundog and believe it or not, this is the least important element, the most important being steadiness. If you do ever make it out on a shoot you'll understand why; you can walk around and pick the birds up yourself if your dog's having a bad day or is learning his trade but if your dog isn't steady on the field you won't be invited back until he is, that is, if you're invited back at all.

Whenever I start training a dog to retrieve, no matter how old the dog is, I want the dog to enjoy the experience and do it enthusiastically. With puppies it is more about sitting on the kitchen floor and being really exciting; with a grown up dog, however, especially a dog that has learned he can outrun me and can't be caught if he doesn't want to be, teaching a retrieve on the long line keeps it fun for the dog and stress free (or at least relatively stress free) for the owner.

So. You have your dog, you have your long line and you have your toy; try to use a toy that is big enough so that you can hold it at the same time as your dog. I'd say you were ready to start.

Hold your dog by your side with the long line laid out at the side of you. Send your dog as soon as the toy lands or even slightly before - as you send your dog say your usual fetch word followed immediately with "get on"; if you don't have a fetch word just use "get on". When your dog picks up the item say "hold" and call your dog interspersing "come" with "good boy, hold".

Crouch down or kneel and, keeping your hands in close to your body, give verbal praise and encouragement, then as your dog comes within your space stroke him and scratch him and give him masses of fuss, then quietly with one hand take hold of his collar and with the other hand put your hand on the toy and say "dead" or "give" and take the toy from him. If he doesn't relinquish it straight away let go of his collar and remove the toy from his mouth.

Do not expect your dog to sit or in any way be formal at this stage in the training, keep it fun, keep it exciting and it will keep your dog wanting more.

What if it doesn't go according to plan?

Well the first thing that can go wrong is your long line. A fantastic training tool but can get tangled and worse still can get tangled behind you and pull you over. It's really important before you send your dog that you make sure your line isn't tangled at all and that you're not in danger of standing on it as you move or that the dog doesn't take the whole line with him as you send him for the retrieve, rather it should ribbon out behind him.

What if, when your dog gets to the toy he doesn't want to pick it up? What if he wanders off to sniff something instead? This is why, as suggested earlier you start your training wherever possible indoors or some really boring place that doesn't have many yummy smells.

• If your dog isn't interested in the toy you need to do one of a few things... first and foremost check your dog doesn't need the toilet, then think about how you threw the toy – were you exciting? If you've got a dog that's not overly playful you have to whip them up in their excitement so that their eyes are gleaming and they can't wait for you to release them to get the toy. With your dog beside you do a couple of mock throws making silly noises as you do then throw it for real letting your dog run in as you throw it (this is known as 'taking off the brakes').

• Do you play with your dog? If not you need to start playing with toys with your dog. Once you've taught your dog to 'leave it' there's no reason why you can't play pull providing you follow these rules; when you say "give" your dog hands over the toy immediately, your dog never gets away with snatching the toy from your hands, your dog is never allowed to grab the toy (or anything else for that matter) uninvited, all toys belong to you.

• And then there is the toy itself. Make it an exciting toy for them to retrieve; using a squeaky initially isn't a good idea as it may encourage him to crunch down to squeak the toy on the way back – great for playing but not teaching the retrieve, saying that, if your dog doesn't like any other toy make it an unusual shape squeaky something like a folded up newspaper for example. An Air or Wubba Kong is perfect for teaching the retrieve as it's a good size for the dog to hold and has a 'tail' which makes it easy to throw and get hold of whilst in your dog's mouth.

Hold your dog by your side with the long line laid out at the side of you;
make sure the line is untangled and away from your feet

*Send your dog as soon as the toy lands or even slightly before, with a "get on".
Keep your arm outstretched until your dog gets to the toy*

*When your dog picks up the toy say "hold" and give plenty of verbal praise and encouragement. Remember
to keep your hands in close to your body*

- Go and get the toy yourself and bring your dog back to the original position. Be exciting as you throw the toy. As your dog approaches the toy say "what's that then?"/"what you got?"/"come on then bring it here" (or words to that effect) in an excited voice and when he picks it up pat your legs and encourage him back. If he doesn't pick it up don't stress, go out to the toy pick it up, have a two second game of pull and throw it a couple of feet away, as he goes to get it encourage him and walk backwards. Repeat this if you have to. When your dog has retrieved, even if it's only a couple of feet, praise him and call it a day then go round the house and collect every single toy and chew that you can find, put them in a box and only bring them out when you're training... your dog has too much access to too many things and thinks "why should I pick it up, I can do that anytime", basically thinking you're not important enough to take any notice of. This is one of the basic principles of dog ownership, too many toys lying around and the dog will potentially become immune to them, immune to you or possessive over them. Much better to have one or two down for your dog to do with as he pleases and the rest put aside for you to use to initiate play, but if he's not retrieving then take them all away until he does.

What if he dances about and won't bring the toy back? That is why you have your dog on a long line. If, while doing the puppy retrieve, your dog doesn't return, very gently start winding him in on the line while encouraging him to come back to you. It's really important when he comes back not to touch the toy or try to take it off him; that's probably the reason he didn't come back, he wanted to keep the toy either for himself or to entice you into a game of chase (a favourite amongst all canines... and probably all primates too). Just make a big fuss of him and then quietly take the toy. Continue to fuss him once you have the toy firmly in your possession and either put the toy away or do another retrieve; your choice.

If your dog tries running behind you try to train with your back to a wall or train in a hallway if you have one available otherwise turn to face him so that he's never behind you.

Spitting the toy out? Just pick up the toy and either pop it gently into your dog's mouth and wiggle it a little, just enough to encourage your dog to keep it in his mouth (saying "hold" as you do so) and then ask your dog to "give" up the toy after a second or so; or pick the toy up and encourage a two second game of pull and then ask your dog to "give" the toy up. If you do one of the above whenever your dog spits the toy out he'll learn very quickly to hang on to it for you, when he does be exuberant with your praise so that he'll want to hold it in his mouth for you next time.

What's next?

Now that you have your dog retrieving enthusiastically and joyfully, it's time to start to formalise the puppy retrieve.

If your dog is coming straight back and not dicking about you can remove the line, put a shorter less restrictive one on or leave it alone until you're absolutely confident that your dog is going out and back again without distraction. Line your feet up to where you think the toy is going to land; this is where canvas dummies are great as they don't tend to bounce very far on landing. Put the foot that's closest to your dog further back and put your dog into a sit-wait.

Holding on to your dog's collar throw the toy and repeat the wait command. Give it a second or so and as you let go of the collar send your dog saying your usual "fetch" word/"get on" with the other arm outstretched and pointing towards the toy. Keep your arm outstretched and pointing towards the toy until your dog has run well beyond your fingertips.

Remember to say "hold" when your dog picks up the toy and stay crouched or on your knees with your arms in as your dog approaches. Don't try to take the toy until you've given them masses of fuss and then quietly take the item with either a "dead" or "give". As you praise and stroke him calmly pick up the line ensuring he's not going to dick about with the toy or run off with his 'trophy' and do a 'lap of honour' around the sitting room, garden or field.

Formalising the Retrieve

There are many ways to train a retrieve. The way that I prefer is, to be technical for moment, called chaining, that is we train all the various elements as individual exercises and then 'chain' them together. I find that having fun doing the puppy retrieve a couple of times a week (more than 2 but less than 5 retrieves in a row, more than twice but less than 5 times a week is optimum) and spending the rest of the time teaching the more 'formal' elements of it makes for fun balanced training without anyone getting overly stressed about a technique or getting bored with the process.

The retrieve is really made up of five elements; casting off, picking up and holding, the return, the present, returning to heel (the finish), however, puppy retrieve aside we'll teach it in order of the present, the return, the finish, hold and casting off... almost but not quite 'backward chaining'

The present

Rather than overcomplicate things it's much easier to train the present as sitting in front, reasonably close looking up at you. Train it without your dog holding anything in his mouth and be consistent. Over a short period of time whenever you say "come" your dog will sit nicely in front of you... you then progress to doing it with a retrieve article.

Initially, that is until your dog 'gets it' or until we add a retrieve article, we'll be using a combination of treats and corrections as well as the ever present smiles, strokes, scratches and "good boys".

Put your dog in a sit whilst on lead and stand squarely in front of him.

With a treat in your left hand and reasonably short lead held in your right hand, placed midline and low in front of your body, take a small to tiny step backwards and say "come"; as you do so gently flick the lead towards you to encourage your dog to move forwards. When he has moved forward gently tell him to sit (with your hand signal at the same time) and give him the sweetie. Your dog must sit straight and reasonably close.

When you can do this one 'baby' step at a time, try walking backwards using three or four small strides having the dog follow you squarely; as you stop put the dog into a sit and reward.

After a couple of tries take a big step backwards and give your dog a really big scratch/stroke to release. By stepping backwards you're not pushing your dog out of his sit position or making him leap backwards or to the side, it's staying controlled but enjoyable.

When you're happy with how you are both progressing, start withholding the treats and give a sweetie on every third or fourth good, straight sit. If you don't want to use food treats this exercise works just as well using verbal praise instead, you'll learn very quickly what tone of voice works for your dog and what doesn't, regardless though remember to smile at your dog when he gets it right and make sure your smile makes it to your eyes.

With a treat in your left hand and reasonably short lead held in your right hand, take a small to tiny step backwards and say "come"; as you do so gently flick the lead towards you to encourage your dog to move forwards

When he has moved forward gently tell him to sit (with your hand signal at the same time) and give him the treat

Your dog must sit straight and be reasonably close

The return

You want your dog to get into the habit of focussing on you whenever you say their name and then start moving towards you. This little exercise will not only have your dog following you around but, when you say their name as part of the recall or after they've picked up the dummy, they'll automatically start heading in your direction.

This exercise helps enormously when training your dog to come back and is an excellent pre-cursor to training a recall.

When your dog's milling around on lead or not focussed on you; step back and say your dog's name in your normal voice, as you do so give a little flick on the lead. If your dog looks at you talk to him in a cheery voice and walk slowly backwards taking baby to tiny steps. If your dog disregards your voice, keep saying their name and gently flicking as you do. The second your dog looks at you start walking backwards as above.

The aim is to get your dog's attention and maintain it without resorting to food. You're also communicating to your dog that you're not to be ignored; you are in fact irritating your dog into not ignoring you; by walking backwards you're teaching your dog that he must follow or get a consequence. All you'll have to do to encourage your dog to return is to step backwards and say their name.

The finish

The finish is quite simply putting your dog to heel from sitting in front of you. There's a couple of ways to put your dog to heel, popping them round to the left or having them walk behind your legs and tucking in on the left. The former in obedience terms is called the flip finish or the swing depending on the exuberance level of your dog and the amount of energy he puts into it (for my lab it would be a flip finish, my Goldie a swing finish) and the latter is just called around; I presume from "go around behind you".

When training for competition obedience I tend to train the 'go around behind' finish, however, with gundogs I prefer the flip finish. Why? Well I'm training my dogs to work on the field and to be out and back again retrieving as fast as they can on most occasions, by just 'flipping' them to heel they can be scanning the field for downed birds as they go back to the heel position and be back to retrieving quickly. Bearing in mind also, that lots of things are happening on a shoot and I want to make sure I can see my dog at all times, if my dog goes behind me every time he brings back a retrieve prior to going out again I've lost sight of him and he could be 'off' after something that I can't see.

Put your dog in a sit whilst on lead and stand squarely in front of him.

With a treat in your left hand lure your dog out to your left hand side as you step back with your left leg (your right leg shouldn't move). As your dog moves say "go to heel", "good boy go to heel".

As your dog gets behind you draw your dog in and forwards as you step together with your left leg... it will look as if your dog has done an anti-clockwise circle to get to your left leg.

Put your dog into a straight sit by your left leg and reward with the treat. Use your lead if necessary to keep the dog in the correct position.

If you don't want to use treats then do the above but instead of 'luring' your dog with a sweetie use a short'ish lead and guide your dog using verbal praise for encouragement.

Remember to smile at your dog when he's getting it right.

Over time you'll be able to be less obvious in your movements and not step back as far and then you'll be at the point where you won't need to step back, just say "go to heel" and point down your left leg and your dog will pop round to heel. It does take patience, time and plenty of co-ordination but when you get there it looks wonderful and you feel so in control.

Starting with your dog sitting squarely in front of you

With a treat in your left hand, lure your dog out to your left hand side
as you step back with your left leg.
As your dog moves say "go to heel", "good boy, go to heel"

As your dog gets behind you, draw your dog in and forwards
as you step together with your left leg.
Put your dog into a straight sit by your left leg and reward with the treat

The hold

There are many ways to get your dog to 'hold' an item in his mouth. The trained hold is when you put an item (dummy, dumbbell etc.,) in your dog's mouth and tell him to "hold". Sometimes the dog will back off and resist and then you can get into "you will hold it" situation which is never good and generates stress and frustration and really needs expert advice on hand to show you how to do it.

Now you know what it is we'll not go any further down the road of the formally trained 'hold' rather we'll do it the way that meets no resistance and is appropriate for 'distance learning' which is what you're doing now reading this book.

Whenever you throw anything for your dog, from now on, as your dog picks it up say "*dog* hold". Whenever your dog picks something up from choice and carries it in his mouth say "*dog* hold". Whenever your dog brings something to you, just before he drops it say "*dog* hold".

Whenever your dog drops something at your feet or spits things out either, pick the item up, gently pop it in his mouth (be careful not to force it in or push it too far back) and say "hold" and then remove it OR put it close to his mouth wiggling it to encourage him to take it, once it's in his mouth say "hold" and then remove it OR leave it on the floor and encourage him to pick it up, once it's in his mouth say "hold" and then remove it.... you get the idea don't you.

Never accept anything from your dog that has been dropped, only ever engage in play or retrieves if your dog puts the item in your hand.

Whenever your dog picks something up and crunches it give him a different word... I use 'yeeha' which is me saying to my dog that he can do want he wants with the toy, well, actually it means run around like a lunatic with a toy in your mouth. If however, I've asked the dog to retrieve a toy formally and he starts to crunch he gets a firm "no!"

A word of warning with training your dog to holding and the use of food treats. Never, in the early days, give your dog a food reward for holding and retrieving, instead give verbal and physical rewards and praise. Why? Well, your dog can't hold something in his mouth and eat at the same time, the second he thinks there's a food option he will empty his mouth and you've got it, the dummy will hit the ground.

When I first trained my lab to the dummy it was without sweeties, then when I trained him for competition obedience I introduced a treat... that was it, he would quite literally throw the dummy at me three or four paces away. We quickly nipped that one in the bud I can tell you, he will now very politely hold a dummy in his mouth while I balance a sweetie on his forehead. He knows now through consistent training that unless he waits until I take the dummy there's no sweetie... so he waits!

Putting it together

Now you have trained the recall/return, the present and the finish it's time to put these individual exercises together into a smooth chain of events. It means when you move on to the retrieve your dog will have a comfortable picture of what's expected of him when he returns.

First of all put your dog in a sit-wait whilst on lead (ideally 6ft). Walk to the end of the lead and then turn to face your dog; stand parallel to him so that your feet are pointing at his front paws/your pelvis is opposite his pelvis so that you are setting him up to succeed.

With two treats in your left hand at your tummy and your lead in your right, say "come"; as you do so gently flick the lead towards you to encourage your dog to move forwards. When he has come to you gently tell him to sit (with your hand signal at the same time) and give him the sweetie. Your dog must sit straight and reasonably close.

Then step back with your left leg and, using the treat in your left hand lure your dog into the heel position saying "heel" or "come to heel" as you do.

Remember if your dog doesn't come in straight take baby strides backwards and guide him in as you would when training the present.

Build up the distance on a long-line for this exercise and then start to withhold the treat on the return so that your dog only gets a sweetie when he's back in the heel position.

Casting off

Sending your dog for the retrieve, or casting off as it's called, can make the retrieve simple and set your dog up to succeed every time or it can make it awkward for your dog mentally and physically.

Line your feet up to where you think the dummy's going to land. Place the leg that is closest to your dog further back. Put your dog into a 'sit/wait' or 'sit/stay' and hold your dog while you throw the dummy, as it lands say "mark". Give it a second or so and send your dog saying "get on" with an outstretched arm... remember to keep your arm out until your dog's run well past it.

As the dummy hits the ground, the noise it makes will grab your dog's attention and he will look towards the sound and hopefully see the dummy. By saying "mark" as the dummy, or toy, lands you're conditioning the action (of focusing on the landing) to a word (mark) that you can use later as a command.

Now you've got the technique, let's look at the mechanics and the psychology of casting off.

Think of your dog, like any other four legged animal, as having the engine in the back. All propulsion comes from the hind legs, whether that's launching itself over a jump or walking sedately to the fire; all movement for the dog starts in the back end.

As you 'sit' your dog think about where you're planning on throwing your dummy to, ideally you're looking to have the retrieve item lined up with your dog's pelvis so that when your dog launches himself forwards he's travelling in a straight line rather than having to twist once he gets moving. It's much easier to line your dog up nicely for a memory/dropped retrieve rather than a thrown one but it's still worth doing to save your dog any pulled muscles.

The reason for lining your feet up with the dummy or 'pointing' at the dummy with your feet if you like, is to emphasise where you want your dog to go. In time if you want to do more serious training with your dog starting this now will be a godsend, if you don't want to do anything more serious than retrieve on walks and have fun this will still make it easier for your dog to understand what it is you want him to do.

Dogs are the only animal on the planet, other than humans, that can follow the point. Even our closest relative the ape cannot. It is believed that the dogs have taught themselves, after being around humans in such a close setting, that following the point is a good thing. Their cousin the wolf doesn't follow the point, although when hunting in a pack, the pack leader will communicate his intention through his gaze. Dogs will also follow the gaze or eye movement from a human.

So here we are pointing with our hand and our feet at the object of our desire, we've lined our dogs pelvis up to the dummy so that when he launches himself forward for the retrieve he's travelling in a smooth straight line.

Now for the problems...

You say "get on", your dog runs out a couple of paces and then turns around and looks at you. Did you keep your arm outstretched?

I'd be very surprised if you did. Quite often dogs that run out six feet or so then do a circle before continuing have been trained by people that flick their arm out and back when casting off their dog. The dog starts to run and is distracted by the hand being brought back in, whether that's because he thinks he's in trouble or that he's being told to come back in or whether he thinks there's something in the hand I don't know, I've just seen it happen again and again where people don't keep their arm outstretched long enough for the dog to get beyond it.

You say "get on" and your dog runs off to the right and completely ignores the dummy!

Ah, chances are your dog was looking over to the right (or the left if he went that way) and not at the dummy when you gave him his "get on" command.

Once you're all lined up, stop looking at the dummy and instead look down at your dog and see where he's focussed. It's okay, you can, the dummy isn't going anywhere. You should be able to see the top of your dogs head if not his eyes. His brow will be smooth and he should be looking at the dummy. If he's not, don't send him. Instead click your fingers on the hand that's sending him (if he's on your left it will be your right hand) to get his attention and as soon as looks in the right direction, send him. He should now head in the direction of the dummy.

Have the leg closest to your dog further back and point your feet to
where you think the dummy will land

With your arm outstretched towards the dummy, send your dog;
remember to look at your dog rather than the dummy... after all the dummy's not going anywhere!

Stay relaxed and have fun... remember to smile

Almost there

Now you've got your dog running out nicely for a retrieve we need to look at what to do when he brings it back. When your dog picks up the item say "hold" and call your dog immediately, this will get your dog into the good habit of returning promptly. Praise your dog as he's returning and "good hold".

When he's about 6 foot in front of you, slowly walk backward patting your tummy and praising your dog for following you. Step forward, take the dummy and praise your dog. If your dog is coming in off to the side turn the opposite way, still walking backwards and call your dog – as soon as he's straight step forward, take the dummy and praise.

When your dog is consistently coming in straight while walking backwards, stop, tell your dog to 'sit' and take the dummy.

When your dog is happy with this, stop walking backwards and when your dog has picked up the dummy, whistle, pat your tummy and SMILE as your dog comes in, praising him when he gets about 10 foot or so away, encourage your dog in front and 'sit'.

When your dog sits calmly in front of you, smile, reach down and gently take the dummy

The finished product

The most important thing about teaching your dog to retrieve is that it's fun: fun for you and fun for your dog. It may seem as if there's a lot involved, well a lot more than just throwing a toy and letting your dog play fetch with it. There is. We're going for obedience and a way to channel the dogs mind from being scattered to having purpose; remember he has been bred to help you get your lunch and there's nothing that will bring more focus to a gundog than a retrieve.

So, here we go, the retrieve, from the top.....

With your dog sitting to heel, tell him to wait and slide the foot closest to him back and throw the dummy, or the toy, so it lands more or less in front of him although at distance. As it lands say "mark". Tell him to wait again and stretch your arm out towards the dummy then look down at your dog to make sure he's looking in the right direction and cast him off with a "get on".

When your dog has picked up the dummy praise him, whistle him back and

smile. As your dog comes in pat your tummy (are you still smiling?) and tell your dog to sit in front of you. Take the dummy, tell him what a good boy he is and put him to heel, smiling as you do so.

Congratulations you have just done a formal retrieve. Now break off from training and play with your dog!

The Marked Retrieve

A marked retrieve is, quite simply, a retrieve that your dog has seen thrown and has been given the opportunity to 'mark' it.

You start off by throwing it yourself, having your dog 'mark' it and send your dog. You then enlist the help of friends and family. Have them standing opposite you at a distance (initially only as far as you yourself can throw), have them tap/slap the dummy with their free hand to get the dogs attention and make a brruuuppp bbrrruuuuppp kind of noise and throw the dummy up, underarm. The noise they make prior to throwing it will attract your dog's attention. This time as the dummy is in the air and the dog is following it with his eyes say "mark". This will improve your dog's timing and marking ability. In your own time, send your dog.

As your dog is confidently retrieving a dummy from your friend (thrower), have them move further away from you, gradually building up the distance but always bringing it in again after a gap in training. If you increase the distance too quickly your dog will mis-mark it and you'll be setting him up to fail which is the last thing you want. You want your dog to trust your judgement, your training and feel confident and enthusiastic in his retrieves.

When your dog is happy doing one retrieve have your thrower throw one dummy after another. Send your dog for the second dummy thrown and then after he's retrieved it, take your time to set him up again, making sure his pelvis is lined up to the dummy as you place him in a sit.

The reason for retrieving the second dummy first, especially in the early days, is to develop your dog's latent learning skill. The last dummy thrown is the dummy your dog is focussed on and is most likely to get right. It also means he only needs to remember where one dummy is (the first thrown) as he can see, and is focussed on, the second one.

In dogs, humans and every animal in between, latent learning is about learning something and then filing it away for later use. In relation to your gundog it's a quality that is highly valued in working and trials dogs alike and I tend to think of it as your dog taking a Polaroid photo and filing it away for later.

This is another reason why you should try to be precise when setting your dog up to retrieve, it makes it easier for him to find his snapshot of the landscape if he's viewing it from the same position that he took his 'photo' from.

A word of warning when using a thrower to help with your retrieves: don't allow your thrower to whistle to get your dog's attention. The first time I asked my husband to be thrower for me I omitted this instruction. My husband whistled then threw the dummy, I cast off my dog and he galloped over to my hubby and did a beautiful present totally ignoring the dummy... hmmmm, let's not do that again!

The Memory Retrieve

The memory retrieve is also known as the dropped retrieve and is used, not only to make it more interesting for your dog, but to improve his ability to mark items at distance and, as you increase the complexity of the memory retrieve you further develop his latent learning skills.

Pop your dog to heel and walk out ten or so strides. Pat the dummy and make your brrrruuuppping noise and drop the dummy on the ground. Do an about turn to the left and walk back the way you came. When you get back to where you started do another left about turn and line your dog's pelvis up with the dummy. When he's straight, pop him in a sit and cast him off for the retrieve as you've taught him.

For this exercise I tend to use a left about turn (left turn then left turn as described in 'walking on a loose lead') rather than a right about turn. Why? Well if you were to do a right about turn as you put the dummy down, as you turn away from the dummy your dog could duck out on the turn and pick the dummy up. This is more likely to happen when doing this exercise on a long line or off lead rather than when training on a regular slip. As always set your dog up to succeed in everything and do a left about turn.

By going back to the same position you're giving your dog a sense of familiarity and, once you've trained this exercise a couple of times your dog will learn to 'put together' the landscape with the dropped dummy so as you turn him prior to sending him he'll pull together the picture he had in his mind as you set off to drop the dummy with the picture of the dummy being dropped. That along with his body being pointed in the right direction will contribute to a focussed, enthusiastic retrieve.

Once you're both comfortable doing this exercise at ten paces increase it to twelve and then fifteen and so on, never increase the distance by more than two to three strides as you're developing a skill and if you increase the distance too much too soon your dog quite simply won't see the dummy and will be reluctant to leave your side or lose confidence on the way and stop. Do this often enough and your dog will lose confidence in your handling ability also.

Upping the Ante...

The next stage in your dogs training is to introduce the clock. Not a stopwatch, although if you've decided you quite fancy a scurry at the next Game-fair then it's worth finding out just how fast your dog is, no this is using the image of the clock face in your mind as you train your dog.

Imagine you're in the centre of the clock face, heel your dog to the 12 o'clock position and drop a dummy remembering to tell your dog to 'mark' the position; then left about turn and heel to the 6 o'clock position and drop another dummy, again remembering to tell your dog to 'mark' the position; then left about turn and heel back to the centre of the clock face, where you started from. Pop your dog in a sit (you should be facing 12 o'clock and the first dummy down) and then, when your dog sees the dummy, send your dog.

When your dog has retrieved the first dummy and you've put him nicely to heel, do a left about turn more or less on the spot so you end up facing the 6 o'clock position and pop your dog in a sit. Once again when your dog sees the dummy send your dog and while doing so put your dummy either under your arm, in your pocket or dropping it quietly behind you.

Initially I would make the clock between 30 to 40 paces across so that when you're in the centre it's about 15 to 20 paces to each dummy. As you increase the complexity of the exercise remember to decrease the distance of the retrieve to ensure your dog keeps a high level of confidence in you and himself.

When you've enjoyed playing with 12's and 6's and feel ready to move on add in 3 o'clock and 9 o'clock. This time walk a large circle with your dog to heel and as you pass the points on the clock face drop a dummy. When all four dummies are down, walk to the centre of the clock and set your dog up to retrieve them in the order you choose.

You can also use the clock face to increase your dog's steadiness and rather than walk out to place the dummies down, pop your dog in a sit stay and throw the dummies into position. Return to your dog's side and using the skills you've learned so far, turn your dog on the spot to line him up to dummies and retrieve as usual.

Remember to take it slowly and if your dog makes a mistake have a think about whether you've gone too fast for him, in which case go back a step in your training; whether he doesn't understand what's expected of him, in which case go back a step in your training or whether he's dicking about in which case it's back to training the basics of 'come', 'present' and 'finish to heel' and working him back on the long line.

The Blind Retrieve

The blind retrieve is, as the name implies, sending your dog to retrieve an item that he hasn't seen being put down. Before you can send your dog on a blind retrieve he has to trust you that there's something there for him to go find.

Everything that you've learned and taught your dog has led you to this point; a relationship that's been built on leadership and trust.

Before we go any further with the blind retrieves there's another command you need to train your dog. You'll love this one; it's great fun, although you probably won't love it as much as your dog. You need to train your dog to use his nose on command. The command or the words that I use are "find it". Other trainers use different words and as always that choice lies with you the trainer, if you want to use another word please do; field trialists tend to use "hi-lost" and the people I regularly shoot with use "where is it" (although it sounds like "weeeeeesit") and others "get it".

Find it!

The easiest way to train your dog to use his nose is to give him something worth using his nose for. For me you can't beat digestive biscuits for this exercise. They smell delicious, they crumble easily and dogs just can't get enough of them, even the fussy eaters.

This exercise is best taught on grass. Armed with a couple of digestives, put your dog in a sit-wait. Walk a couple of paces in front of him, repeat the wait command and crumble a bit of biscuit. Release your dog from the wait and as he comes forward point to the crumbs. As he sniffs the ground say "find it", "good boy find it". Do this a couple of times and then, as he's in his sit-wait, lay out a couple of piles of crumbs a couple of feet apart. Release him from his wait and point to the first lot of crumbs saying "find it" as he's snuffling for them, then, as he's finished, point to the second lot of crumbs encouraging him over and telling him to "find it" again.

Do this little exercise a couple of times a day for a week and at the end of the week you'll have a dog that drops his nose to the ground sniffing when you point down and say "find it".

I can remember teaching this exercise a few years ago to one of my gundog groups. When we'd finished it and went to move on to another exercise I turned quickly and all the digestive biscuits flew out of the top my bag as I hadn't resealed the packet properly. The dogs, being gundogs, marked where they landed and, even though we picked them all up and moved to a different part of the field, when we sent the dogs out to retrieve the dummies, every single one that was sent made a beeline for where the biscuits landed and you could hear them sniffing and snuffling trying to find them. Take note and only train "find it" at the end of a training session!

Training in the home

The most fun way to teach a blind retrieve is playing hide and seek in the home, only hide and seek with a toy or a dummy rather than you hiding, especially after you've taught the 'find it' command.

Take a favourite toy or dummy and then put your dog in one room and close the door. If you're at the point where you've trained your dog to sit-stay while you're out of the room do that otherwise leave your dog with a 'not you' and close the door behind you. Go and hide the toy in another room in a very simple place, maybe behind an open door or round the side of the settee... hidden but in view, if you know what I mean.

Return to your dog and let him out of the room pointing to the room you've just hidden their toy in, say "go find it" and walk with them to the room. Once in the right room, if your dog is looking puzzled say in an excited voice "where's your toy?" he probably won't have a clue what you're saying but will pick up on the energy you put behind it. Point to where the toy is and say "find it", "find your toy". As soon as your dog finds the toy make a really, really big fuss of him. Then it's back to the room you started in and do the exercise exactly the same, putting the toy in the same position as last time. This time when you let him out of the room with a "go find it" he'll know where to look, will find the toy immediately and will feel very pleased with himself... you will be following him making sure he goes in the right direction and saying "find it" as he starts to get close to the toy.

It's up to you if you do it again in the same place or set the toy up in a different room. Providing you're consistent in your approach your dog will very, very quickly pick up that when you say "find it" and point, your dog will find something good if he uses his nose in the area that you're pointing towards.

Do you remember the hotter-colder game you played as a child, where someone would hide something and you had to find it with them saying "warm", "warmer", "hot", "hotter", or "cold", "colder", "freezing"? Well this is the same, the closer your dog gets to finding the toy the more excited your voice gets and the closer together the 'find its' become.

Right then, now who wants to go hunting?

So far we've looked at training lots of individual exercises and putting them together into more training exercises, for example putting the retrieve together with the present and finishing to heel, the sit-wait with the recall and so on; all trained in relative isolation under the banner of training.

But what about the 'real world'?

Well, remember this "there is no such thing in a dog's mind that equates with 'going for a walk'. He goes hunting..." and now he can; he can go hunting for you, on your behalf. He'll be focussed on you watching and waiting for you to send him to retrieve your lunch.

Walking your dog never has to be the same again. Always have a little tug toy or reward toy in your pocket for your dog, a little ball on a rope is great as it fits nicely in the hand and in the pocket. Take a retrieve item with you, a larger toy, a dummy or the ever useful tennis ball.

As you're walking drop the toy and when you get a little way away from it turn around and send your dog for the retrieve. Not only are you satisfying your dogs innate needs but you're having your dog 'hunt' for you and he's getting more exercise than he would normally do by running back and forwards retrieving and you're strengthening your relationship with your dog.

If you live in an area where there are bushes, pop your dog in a sit-wait and put the dummy at the bottom of the bush and send your dog to retrieve it. As your dogs confidence increases put it behind the bushes, send your dog and use the "find it" command as he gets in the right area. In time place the dummy in the bush just slightly off the ground so he learns to look in the less than obvious places for the scent.

Don't want to carry a whole load of 'stuff' out with you on walks? Nah I don't blame you, I quite often will drop a glove or my hat and send my dogs back to retrieve them for me. It means that they're working on my behalf, I don't have to carry extra things on walks with me and if I ever do drop a glove by accident on a walk I can send my dog back for it knowing he'll find it for me.

I don't restrict the items to just hats, gloves and scarves. I have taught both of my dogs, and the dogs that train with me, to retrieve mobile phones and car keys; you can see how handy this is starting to become can't you? A word of warning with keys, put them on a soft key ring for your dog to pick up and pop them inside a sock or a glove to start off with and just have the soft key ring hanging out (I have a 'cuddly' Eeyore toy on mine for this reason). If your dog gallops back like a little rocket then the swinging of the keys may catch him; the glove or sock will protect his face and teach him to slow down and be steady whenever keys are on the retrieve 'menu'.

In the home, as well as hiding toys, we'll get our dogs to take the mail to each other, carry the remote control from one person to another and at Christmas and birthdays they'll carry presents for us.

There are only two restrictions on the fun you can have with your pet gundog, the first is that whatever you do doesn't hurt him or put him at risk and the second is your imagination.

The more you line yourself up with the dummy, the more enthusiastic your dog will be to get it

About the Author

Lez Graham works full-time as a canine behaviour practitioner and gundog trainer, is a registered assessor with the Gundog Club, is the Education & Development Officer for the Guild of Dog Trainers and is a tutor with the Cambridge Institute of Dog Behaviour & Training.

A dog behaviour specialist with a penchant for gundogs, Lez runs weekly gundog training classes. As a gundog trainer, Lez focuses on steadiness and obedience and, by bringing the behaviour element into her gundog training, her handlers get a deeper understanding of why we train the gundog the way we do. Moving away from the 'old-style/traditional' gundog training and yet keeping the discipline of the well trained field dog; she encourages play and touch to facilitate a strong bond between dog and handler.

Lez has competed in Gundog field tests in New Zealand, competition obedience and 'works' both of her gundogs during the shooting season.

Lez is a full member of the Canine and Feline Behaviour Association (CFBA), a master trainer with the Guild of Dog Trainers (GoDT) and is currently studying for her Masters Degree in Dog Behaviour & Psychology with Middlesex University.

Lez lives in Wiltshire with her husband, her son and her two gundogs.

Useful contacts

**The British Association
for Shooting & Conservation
(BASC)**
www.basc.org.uk

The Gundog Club
www.thegundogclub.co.uk

The Kennel Club
www.thekennelclub.org.uk

Dog Training
and Behaviour
**The Cambridge Institute
of Dog Behaviour & Training**
www.cidbt.org.uk

**The Canine & Feline Behaviour
Association of Great Britain**
www.cfba.co.uk

The Guild of Dog Trainers
www.godt.org.uk

Equipment
Quest Gundog Training Equipment
www.questgundogs.co.uk

Game fairs
Countryman Fairs
www.countrymanfairs.co.uk

Living Heritage
www.livingheritagecountryshows.co.uk

Scurry Bandits
www.scurrybandits.org

Lez' sites
Lez Graham
www.lezgraham.com

The Pet Gundog
www.thepetgundog.co.uk

Trained for Life
www.trainedforlife.co.uk

Photography
Nick Ridley Photography
www.nickridley.com

Shooting
**Lains Shooting School
& Mullenscote Gundogs**
www.lainsshootingschool.co.uk